# HOLY DISOBEDIENCE

# Holy Disobedience
## *When Christians Must Resist the State*

Lynn Buzzard
Paula Campbell

SERVANT BOOKS
Ann Arbor, Michigan

Copyright © 1984 by Lynn Buzzard and Paula Campbell
All rights reserved

Published by Servant Books
P.O. Box 8617
Ann Arbor, Michigan 48107

Book design by John B. Leidy
Cover photo by John B. Leidy © 1984 Servant Publications

Printed in the United States of America
ISBN 0-89283-184-7

84 85 86  10 9 8 7 6 5 4 3 2 1

**Library of Congress Cataloging in Publication Data**

Buzzard, Lynn Robert.
  Holy disobedience.


  Bibliography: p.
1. Government, Resistance to—Religious aspects—
Christianity.  I. Campbell, Paula.  II. Title.
BV630.2.B89  1984    261.7    84-14105
ISBN 0-89283-184-7

# Contents

# ONE

# Holy Disobedience?

*We must be an aggressive, feisty, dig-in-your-heels, kick-and-scream bunch.*                    Franky Schaeffer III

A NATIONAL JOURNAL IN 1980 DECLARED, "The stage is set for a clash between religion and statecraft." Little did they perhaps realize that the clash would not be mere struggles over competing political policies, but be perceived as a war, even a holy war. They weren't alone in missing the trends. Terence Bell, professor of political science at the University of Minnesota, wrote in 1973 that after the civil rights struggles and the Vietnam War protests of the 60s, civil disobedience was "interesting" and raised "theoretical questions," but was "now largely passe."

In the 80s, the issue of civil disobedience has emerged again, though in a radically different context. Perhaps, when Rosa Parks refused to move to the back of the bus she set the stage for a whole new style of American social and political life. Adlai Stevenson declared that "even a jail sentence is no longer a dishonor but a proud achievement. Perhaps we are destined to see in this law-loving land, people running for office not on their stainless records, but on their prison records." William Booth seemed to concur, indicating that "No great cause ever achieved a triumph before it furnished a certain quota to the prison population."

Who would have thought, though, that political and religious conservatives, those who resisted the flower children and peace-niks and praised the draft and "get-tough policies" would become advocates of civil disobedience? These groups historically defended the status quo, citing the biblical duty to obey authorities which are ordained by God (Rom 13). Yet, in surprising numbers, they have begun to leave their comfortable pews and take to the streets with their more liberal religious colleagues, albeit on different issues. Agreeing with Thomas Jefferson that "a strict observance of the written laws is doubtless one of the high duties of a good citizen, but it is not the highest," these traditional conservatives, are pointing to the sovereignty of God and insisting, like Peter, that "we must obey God not man" (Acts 5:29). They have begun to challenge the very authority which, only a decade ago, they described as God's ordained servant.

Most Christians are not about to challenge the school board, much less Caesar. But a growing and vocal group are fed up, angry, and deeply disturbed about American society. They are willing to risk confrontation. One spokesman for a conservative religious group warned "No more Mr. Nice Guy!"

## The Targets

The targets for civil resistance are multiple. One primary concern is the "American Holocaust"—abortion. An aide indicated in private conversations that Jerry Falwell has considered chaining himself to the White House fence. Francis Schaeffer suggested that Christians might at some point refuse to pay a portion of taxes which support abortion. "It's time," he declared, "for Christians and others who do not accept the narrow and bigoted humanist views rightfully to use the appropriate forms of protest."[1] The Moral Majority has suggested using that tactic if the Human Rights Amendment did not pass. Schaeffer's son, Franky, is tougher; he calls for "militant indifference to the edicts of mere men when they contradict God's law."[2] Many have spoken of the possibility of "kidnapping" a baby left to die, such as Baby Doe in Indiana, to preserve the life of the child. One group has already gone beyond words. The Army of God kidnapped operators of an abortion clinic in southern Illinois.

This is not the abstract rhetoric of cultural outcasts. Recently in Grand Rapids, Michigan, the Honorable Randall J. Hekman, Judge of the Juvenile Court, was petitioned to grant permission for a pregnant thirteen-year-old to obtain an abortion. Judge Hekman refused. He also refused to assign the case to another judge. In the interim the young girl changed her mind and, relying upon her mother's advice and help, bore her child. Hekman was extensively criticized in the press and by judicial colleagues. Hekman explained his "judicial disobedience":

> Are there ever instances in which, for the sake of justice, judges should disobey the law? Or do we want our judges always to behave like mindless bureaucrats who dutifully process cases oblivious to the demands of ultimate justice?
>
> What if the law requires a judge to order the execution of a person known to be totally innocent? What if a judge is required by law to order Jewish people to concentration camps or gas chambers because the law says that Jews are non-persons? What if a judge, sitting on a case involving a runaway slave, disagrees with the Supreme Court's 1856 decision in which black slaves were ruled to be nothing more than chattels? Are these not all instances in which judges should take a stand against unjust laws for the sake of doing that which is ultimately right?
>
> Can the judges in these cases escape moral culpability either by obeying the law and saying they were "just following orders" or by disqualifying themselves so that

other judges without their scruples can issue the unjust decree?

Certainly the "just following orders" defense did not work to excuse the Nazi war criminals—nor should it have worked.

How about disqualification? If a judge steps aside from a case knowing full well that another judge will be found who is appropriately "unbiased" and who thus will enforce the unjust law, the first judge does not absolve himself from his moral dilemma. The judge who is required by law to order the execution of an innocent man who deliberately gives the case to another judge remains a knowing and willing part of the ultimate injustice. . . .

I trust that most people would agree with the above in theory. But does this principle apply in a case where a judge is asked to order the killing of an unborn child because the thirteen-year-old mother who is five months pregnant feels this is what she wants? I believe, without question, it does. Let me explain why.

Ten short years ago, a judge in Michigan would be guilty of a felony crime if he encouraged, much less ordered that a pregnant girl obtain an abortion. Then, in 1973, the Supreme Court ruled that all state laws making abortion a crime were unconstitutional. In one day, that which had been a reprehensible crime became a sacred right protected by the Constitution itself.

But not only has the Supreme Court made what was formerly illegal and unthinkable a constitutionally revered and protected right, it has given to trial judges the responsibility not merely to protect this right for women, but actually to order the killing of the unborn. The Supreme Court never had to order that an abortion take place, only that women could choose an abortion if they so desired. But juvenile court judges, whose statutory responsibility is the protection of children from abuse, must perform the "hatchet job" of assigning unborn children to a cruel and merciless death when their mothers are immature and cannot legally make the decision for themselves. What is equally absurd is that, in considering whether to order the demise of an unborn baby, judges are required to engage in the mental fiction that the baby is a nonentity.

Is not the case where a judge is asked to order the killing of an unborn child almost identical to our earlier example where a judge is asked to order the execution of a totally innocent man? I say it is. When faced with this issue, a judge should courageously do what is ultimately right and just by resisting the action which is requested. Transferring the case to another judge will only make the first judge an "aider and abetter" of the ultimate injustice.... We have a majority of the U.S. Supreme Court arbitrarily legalizing the killing of unborn babies based on their own subjective predilections and apart from written legal principles.

The obvious question is: when did the American people give their "public servants" sitting on the U.S. Supreme Court the authority to make these arbitrary absolutes that so affect the lives of the unborn? The answer is that, unless the Court has acquired squatter's rights over time, they have never been given this authority.[3]

Richard and Sheila Reeder took Schaeffer's tax suggestion. In 1980 and 1981, they reduced their taxes in the amount of 1½ percent, declaring in court documents that "at the root of our dispute is the governmental support of abortion and associated programs which are estimated to comprise 1½ percent of the federal budget. We cannot in good conscience support such, so we reduced our taxes by that amount when filing our 1979 and 1980 returns." Noting that the amount deducted in each of the affected years was approximately $100, but that they have been assessed $12,000, the Reeder's insisted "the additional $12,000 in dispute is simply the result of arbitrary and capricious action by the IRS, harassment in attempt to intimidate us, action more representative of Germany and Soviet Russia than the United States." In a separate letter to Mr. Kenneth C. Johannsen of the Internal Revenue Service, Mr. Reeder declared:

> The Bible teaches clearly that Christians are to obey *lawful* authority and it is sinful to not do so. The Bible teaches equally clearly that it is sinful to obey men when they seriously contravene the laws of God. Both principles were upheld at the Nuremberg war trials. Now, abortion and associated practices are clearly contrary to God's law. Thus I cannot in good conscience stand idly by while my taxes are used for such purposes.

## Padlocked Church!

Perhaps the most flamboyant and well-publicized recent case involves the resistance by fundamentalist pastors in Nebraska. That state has tried to close down private Christian schools which refused, on religious grounds, to comply with state requirements that teachers be from state-approved schools. Everett G. Sileven, pastor of the Faith Baptist Church in Louisville, Nebraska, has become something of a folk hero. He lectured throughout the United States while warrants called for his arrest in Nebraska. For its small private school of twenty-nine pupils, the church unsuccessfully challenged the regulations in state and federal courts, claiming the state's regulations were impermissible interference with the free exercise of religion. The church also refused to close down the school when so ordered by a court. Law enforcement officials arrested Sileven in the church and padlocked the doors. Television cameras whirred as the pastor was arrested in the church, children watched in amazement, and the congregation sang hymns. Wide publicity was given to the court order padlocking the church except for specified worship times.

The church worked hard to distribute pictures of. the padlocked door. They seemed to have heeded Kent Kelley who had written, "Get on your knees. Get out the bible. Meet the attorneys. Meet the issues. But don't forget to meet the press!"⁴ If the publicity was supposed to rally public opinion, it did not work. One disgusted local resident, Dayton Hennings, insisted that "a rope and a shotgun would help." Polls showed most state residents opposed the church's actions. State officials complained of high pressure tactics and harassment of state authorities by late night phone calls.

A parade of pastors and conservative religious leaders from over thirty states came to Nebraska to defend those they believed were their persecuted brethren. For a time, the church operated the school across state lines. Fathers were jailed for refusing to testify about school operations and warrants were issued for wives who fled the state. In April of 1984, new legislation seemed to offer relief, and Everett Sileven returned and was held in contempt of court and began serving a jail term.

Congressman George Hansen of Idaho declared that "after Nebraska, we don't need an appeal to some prophetic visionary like George Orwell. It's already happening."

Events such as those in Louisville in 1983 have intensified both the rhetoric and the reflection. A fundamentalist group of activists met in Chicago August 8 and 9 to hold a "Symposium On Theology and Methods of Christian Resistance." In a news release describing themselves as an "ad hoc Committee on Christian Resistance" the group noted their "apprehensions concerning the current turn of government in the United States toward humanism and its tenets, and the shift towards repression of traditional religious liberty." They adopted a "declaration of grievances" to government officials which listed twenty-three items. They concluded:

We are not men of war, but we have suffered intolerable tyranny from bureaucrats and judges. Our patience has been stretched to its limit. Restore the constitutional liberties and prerogatives of our churches or face an outraged, an activist clergy ready to mount a biblically and constitutionally consistent counter-offensive to regain those liberties.

In September 1983, concerned pastors organized the American Coalition of Unregistered Churches. The founders spoke of preparation for "whenever the crest of the wave of tyranny breaks."

The private school issue is far from the only one that has created activists in the conservative camp. The recent extension of Social Security to churches has similarly created a group bent on resistance. Gary Bergel of Intercessors for America speaks of tax resistance in the context of Social Security taxes on church employees. "If our forefathers resisted a tax on *tea,* what would they do with this?" The National Christian Action Council Coalition's newsletter *Alert* suggests that our founders would have resisted such a tax.

The battle over government licensing of religious day care centers and other ministries has also been quite intense. For years, Lester Roloff defied orders of the Texas Department of Human Resources to license his three child care homes in the state. Roloff insisted that his religious convictions prevented him from obtaining a license from the state since that would grant the state's authority to control the church. "No one can license my faith," insisted Roloff. "We don't need to be accredited by a failing humanistic system that has no Christ, no Bible, no God, and no standard." Roloff later won a court battle.

Another area of conservative protest has been resistance to home education restrictions. Hundreds of parents are apparently defying state laws regarding limits on or prohibitions of home education.

In one Western state, another issue surfaced when many pastors indicated that they would not comply with a new state law requiring them to report possible cases of child abuse. They insisted it would violate clergy confidentiality.

There is, of course, the usual number of unique and unusual cases of individual dissent to government regulation. In Wooster, Ohio, members of the Old Order Amish sect have refused to secure the county's $55 building permits, claiming that such permits would violate their religion. Henry Herschberger has been fined $5,000 for refusing to get a permit, though the county will give him $280 credit for two weeks he spent in jail. "If they take the shirts off our backs, that's up to them," Herschberger says. "We won't fight them. We consider the religion more important than a court order." The county plans to auction off fifteen of Herschberger's seventeen cows to collect the remaining $4,720.

Consider the story of Royston Potter. He was fired by the Murry Police Department in suburban Salt Lake City, Utah, when they discovered Potter, a Brigham Young University graduate, had two wives. Potter, pointing to a Bible declared, "that is what I base everything on." Potter is among what some have estimated to be perhaps 20,000 Utahans, mostly Morman fundamentalists, who continue to practice polygamy. The twenty-nine-year-old Potter has sued local officials for dismissing him.

## *A Popularizer of Resistance*

The legitimacy of civil disobedience on the part of Evangelicals and orthodox Christians has been given a substantial boost by the recently deceased Francis Schaeffer. He has become one of the most respected advocates of civil resistance among evangelicals. In 1976, Schaeffer wrote, "Let us not forget why the Christians were killed. They were *not* killed because they worshipped Jesus. . . . Nobody cared who worshipped whom as long as the worshipper did not disrupt the unity of the state, centered in the formal worship of Caesar. The reason Christians were killed was because they were rebels."[5] More recently, he has put the issue even more clearly: "There is a bottom line that must be faced squarely if the state is not to become all powerful and to serve God's primacy." He concludes that Christians must resist unjust and immoral authorities, perhaps even to the point of using force, because the ultimate issue is one of sovereignty: "If there is no place for Civil Disobedience, then the government has been made autonomous, and as such it has been put in the place of the living God."[6]

Schaeffer's *Christian Manifesto* has been widely distributed. The New York Patriot's Society said that it will "shake up today's church." They urge: "Buy it for your friends who hide behind Romans 13." Jerry Falwell's Old Time Gospel Hour alone has distributed 62,000 copies.

Schaeffer's newest volume, *The Evangelical Disaster,* warns that the unwillingness of major biblically committed institutions to risk confrontation with secularism and government has set them on a course to the loss of their integrity.

In 1983, two new volumes were published in a series *Christianity in Civilization: The Theology of Christian Resistance* and *Tactics of Christian Resistance.* Exploring the biblical and philosophical perspectives on civil disobedience, these constituted a "how-to" manual. The language was not restrained. Allen Stang declared:

The most important war now being fought has yet to be mentioned by network news. . . . We are familiar with the war between Britain and Argentina from the legal issues involved down in the personal stories of the troops. We have been told on a daily basis about the disaster in Lebanon.

The war your reporter speaks of is being fought in the United States. It is a religious war as profound as any recorded in Scripture or history. It is a war that one side appears ready to fight to the death; but which the other isn't yet fully aware it is in. It is a war in which preachers already have been thrown into jail as was Paul: in which preachers have been quite literally dragged from the pulpit. It is a war in which God's people are systematically being brutalized by the satanic instrumentality called the Internal Revenue Service. That issue is the first and most important issue: who should sit upon the highest throne.[7]

The Internal Revenue Service has often come under attack. Its investigatory practices are frequently cited as illustrations of government power run amuck. In fact, its practices have led to a bill introduced by Representative Mickey Edwards (entitled The Church Audit Procedures Act) to limit IRS powers in investigating church finances. The IRS actions in regard to the Church of Christian Liberty in Brookfield, Wisconsin, led to an appeal to the United States Supreme Court. In his brief on behalf of the church, Counsel Joseph Weigel, told the Supreme Court:

> To allow the Seventh Circuit decision to stand would be to provide that the IRS is free any time and anywhere to demand of any church the production of every written document relating to any aspect of church belief or activity, including membership and contributor lists. This is a monstrous and unprecedented invitation to tyranny . . . it lays out a red carpet for the IRS for systematic and mendacious harrassment that King George III at his most villainous could only have viewed with envy, and that Adolf Hitler did not achieve until his dictatorship was totally secure. It grants big brother an unrestricted license to pry into and profane what are, by very definition, the most sacred of men's beliefs and practices without probable cause . . . we believe that such a decision is without precedent in the American Jurisprudence and must be reversed.

The Supreme Court refused to hear the case. For Allen Stang the response to action of this sort is clear. "So what should we do? We should be willing to flood the jails. We should fight to get in. We should get on line. We should overload the circuits. In short, we should keep the faith, and stay the course. If we don't, believers and others will rightly believe our words are a farce."[8] Rousas Rushdoony puts it just as strongly. "The fact is that religious liberty is dead and buried; it needs to be resurrected."[9]

Gary North and David Chilton declared, "We are in a fight. There will be winners and losers. On the day of judgment there will be no prisoners." North warns, "This war is going to escalate, as it has escalated in the past. The question is, will Bible believing churches fight? Will they count the costs? Will they pay the price?"[10]

## *Civil Disobedience Is No Respecter of Ideology*

The war against wars is going to be no holiday excursion or camping party.                                  William James

It is not only the conservatives and the fundamentalists in the religious community who have been advocates and practitioners of civil disobedience. Such methodologies have always had greater appeal to liberals. Groups like the Sojourners Fellowship have given increased space to civil disobedience in their publication. The May 1983 lead article, entitled "A Higher Loyalty," cites approvingly Muste's comment that "noncomformative, holy disobedience, becomes a virtue, indeed a necessary and indispensable measure of spiritual self-preservation, in a day when the impulse to conform, to acquiese, to go along, is used as an instrument to subject men to totalitarian rule and involve them in permanent war." Jim Wallis insists that "a clear call needs to be issued that puts forth the theological legitimacy, even imperative, for Christian civil disobedience in the face of escalating preparations for nuclear war." Echoing Schaeffer's insistence that the issue is one of sovereignty, the issue for Wallis is one of "worship, idolatry, and ultimate loyalty." The issue is "what do we owe to whom."[11]

Wallis put action to his words. On Pentecost Sunday 1983, 3,000 clergy and church leaders gathered in Washington, D.C. As Wallis described it in his later newsletter, "strengthened with song, prayer and scriptural exhortations, 242 of us entered the rotunda of the U.S. Capitol to make a witness for peace. We turned the rotunda into a sanctuary, filled with gospel songs and prayers for peace. Funding for the MX missile system was being debated by Congress within earshot." Then Wallis proudly declares, "We were arrested for praying for peace. It was the largest mass arrest in Washington D.C. since Vietnam war days." Then, perhaps seeking to link himself to Bonhoeffer and King, he declared, "I am writing this letter from jail where many of us are serving five day sentences."

## Paying for War and Praying for Peace

Not surprisingly, the issues that have triggered civil disobedience on the left, are somewhat different than those on the right. Opposition to nuclear weapons and war has been the chief target of Christian civil resistance on the left. Much of the call has been for tax resistance. Calling for "church war-tax resistance," John K. Stoner declares, "The time is come to say that the good words of the church have not been, and are not enough. The risks, the discipline, the sacrifices, and the steps in good faith which the churches asked of governments and the task of disarmament must now be asked of the church in the obligation of war-tax resistance."[12] While noting that war-tax resistance will be called "irresponsible, anarchistic, unrealistic, suicidal, masochistic, naive, feudal, negative, and crazy," nevertheless he insists "when the dust is settled, it will stand as the deceptively simple and painfully obvious Christian response to the world arms race." Stoner calls on church members to cease paying for the arms race as part of "submission to the Lordship of Christ in the nitty-gritty of history." He declares: "Call it Civil Disobedience if you wish, but recognize that in reality it is divine obedience. It is a matter of yielding to a higher sovereignty."

William Durland, a lawyer and theologian and founder of the Center on Law and Pacifism in Philadelphia, goes a step further than Stoner and provides practical guidelines on resisting the war tax. Suggested tactics have included refusal to pay the 2% tax on telephone bills, claiming excessive dependents, and claiming a peace deduction as a miscellaneous deduction.[13]

Tax resistance has a long American religious tradition going back to the Pennsylvania Quakers who led a movement in 1755 to oppose taxes levied by the British to fight the French and Indian wars. Such resistance was common also among members of the historic peace churches—the Quakers, Mennonites, and Brethren—during the Revolutionary and Civil Wars. Today, the movement, in some ways, is not large; in 1979 the IRS counted only 12,000 protesters out of 60,000,000 federal tax returns. It was Thoreau who suggested that "it is not so important that many should be as good as you, as that there be some absolute goodness somewhere; for that will leaven the whole lump."

Several national organizations have lined up behind war tax refusal. Some 10,000 members annually contribute about $40 each to the Fellowship of Reconciliation, a religious pacifist organization. A World Peace Tax Fund proposal has even been introduced in Congress though it has died in committee in the last five sessions. The plan would create a Peace College to promote the peaceful resolution of world conflict.

A conflict with taxes and the IRS leads to an interesting fallout. Tom Cordaro—a lay minister at St. Thomas Church in Ames, Iowa, who had been holding back his federal income taxes since 1979—was discovered by the Internal Revenue Service. The IRS attempted in vain to attach his bank accounts or property. Since he had none of these, however, the IRS asked leaders of the St. Thomas parish to garnishee his wages, but the parish voted nineteen to zero in December 1983 not to obey the IRS order.

Tax protests are only one means of challenging U.S. military policy. Some young men have expressed their opposition to war by refusing to register for the draft. Enton Eller, son of the well-known Church of the Brethren teacher Vernon Eller, was convicted August 17, 1983, for "knowing and willful" refusal to register. In spite of apparent suggestions even by the court, Eller declined to raise issues of selective prosecution or claim that he had "constructively registered" since the government already had all the information it sought. In testimony during a brief three-and-a-half-hour trial, he indicated that, though he could not objectively prove what God was leading him to do, "I'm completely satisfied it is God's will." Judge James C. Turk observed that he did not know if Eller was a "hero," but "the defense you raised or didn't raise here has made you an honorable person in the eyes of this court."

## Storming the Gates of Hell

The opposition to militarism has moved beyond tax resistance, draft avoidance, and other forms of non-cooperation. Borrowing from Vietnam War protest styles, direct action is increasingly advocated. Jim Wallis declared, "Most startling of all is the way the Christians are converging on the nuclear sites all over the country. They call it moving the geography of worship and prayer."[14]

*Christian Century,* in an article "Storming the Gates of Hell,"[15] described several incidents of direct-action civil disobedience.

In September 1979, at the Rocky Flats Nuclear Weapons Trigger Plant near Denver, Colorado, two dozen Christians sang, six of their group cut through a fence and walked with candles a half mile over the rough terrain to a hill overlooking the bomb factory. There they shared a "liturgy of light." They served six months in Colorado jails for trespassing.

On the Feast of Epiphany in 1980, two who described themselves as "prayer commandos" climbed a fence and entered the Bangor Naval Submarine Base near Seattle, Washington. Early the next morning the two climbed a twelve foot double security fence into the maximum security weapons storage depot, where they proceeded to pray at each of the six nuclear weapons bunkers before being arrested. They served one year in federal prison.

In September of 1980, six men and two women entered General Electric's King of Prussia manufacturing plant near Philadelphia and made their way to the security assembly area where re-entry vehicles for nuclear weapons were awaiting shipment. With hammers some of the peacemakers began to "beat swords into plowshares" while others spilled blood on blueprints. The "Plowshares Eight" were convicted and received three to ten year sentences. *Christian Century* notes that "social political resistance and moral imagination must be linked" and cites Thomas Merton, who in the Cuban missile crisis, had declared, "Christian faith begins at the point where all others stand frozen stiff in the face of the unspeakable." Further, "beginning in the mid 60s, a particular vitality was forged by religious anti-war activists who joined the nonviolent politics of Mahatma Gandhi and Martin Luther King with symbolic actions informed by the biblical-prophetic tradition."

On January 6, 1980, John Clark and Jim Douglas, members of Ground Zero, entered the Trident Base at Bangor, Washington. They engaged in a "nuclear stations of the cross."

At the launching of the USS Georgia, the Navy's fourth Trident submarine, members of the Plowshares group entered the shipyards at Groton, Connecticut. There they painted the numbers "666," the symbol of the Beast in the Book of

Revelation, on the ship. They poured blood on the machinery and unfurled a banner, "Swords into Plowshares, Stop Trident Now."

## Sanctuary

National publicity has also been given the recent sanctuary activities of churches which have harbored illegal aliens from South America. The controversial issue is also the subject of an international film produced by the World Council of Churches titled "Sanctuary." The film pictures the fate of one family caught in the cross-fire of opposing forces and its attempt at resettlement. In mid-1983 UPI reported that at least fifty churches in the United States are committing a federal crime by providing sanctuary to an estimated 500,000 Central American illegal aliens. Renny Golden, founder of the Chicago Religious Task Force, a national clearing house for information on the movement, estimated as many as 70,000 Americans could technically be arrested for harboring illegal aliens. Golden indicated in March 1984 that the movement would go above ground. Golden declared: "We are going above ground because we feel it is no longer safe for the refugees. If they will arrest us for what they consider criminal, then they will have to make public their actions and take many of us." The Rev. Michael McConnell declared that the "North American church was under attack by the U.S. government because the church has decided to live out the gospel," though in fact no action seems to have been taken yet against such churches.

The concept of sanctuary is an ancient one. It has legal precedent in America when slaves were offered escape via the Underground Railroad. But harboring illegal aliens carries a penalty of up to five years in prison and a $2,000 fine.

Reba Place Fellowship in Evanston, Illinois, has organized an "overground railroad" to assist refugees to flee to safety in Canada. Their theme is Psalm 79:11, "Let the groans of the prisoners come before thee; according to thy great power preserve those doomed to die." The church seeks assistance of additional congregations.

To date forty-two public sanctuaries for Central American refugees have been set up in the United States and perhaps 600 other groups have opened private sanctuaries. Verne Jerves, a spokesman for the Immigration and Naturalization Service, declared that the harboring of illegal aliens is a violation of the law. He declared, "We do not want a confrontation and will not force one." Jerves continued, "There is nothing in American law that provides for sanctuary in the church or any place else for someone who is here illegally or guilty of something else."

Several national religious bodies have endorsed the sanctuary concept. In Wisconsin, the Episcopal bishops of Milwaukee and Eau Claire have endorsed the action of the Congregation of St. Francis House which opened its doors to four Salvadoran refugees. The standing committee of the Division of Mission and Ministry of the Lutheran Council in the U.S.A. and the board of Church and Society of the United Methodist Church have also endorsed the concept of sanctuary. But Archbishop John Roach of Minneapolis, president of the National Conference of Catholic Bishops, while deploring the human rights abuses in Latin America, declared he was "absolutely convinced that we make progress by changing laws and not by breaking them."[16]

## International Issue

Nor, of course, is the issue of civil disobedience confined to the religious community in the United States or even the Western democracies. In recent years, Americans have largely given enthusiastic support to the efforts of Solidarity, Lech Walesa's challenge to Polish authorities, and the significant role of the church in Poland. In 1984, American television audiences saw thousands of young people marching in protest at the removal of crucifixes from the schools. They flocked to Poland's most revered Roman Catholic shrine at Czestochowa in a peaceful but emotional protest on March 10. Bishop Franciszek Musiel in a homily at a Garwolin monastery praised the students "fight for the crucifixes." "The church will not retreat," said Bishop Jan Mazur of Sieldce to 4,000 cheering teenagers at Garwolin. Riot police had assembled near one school occupied by 400 protesting students.

In the Soviet Union, Christians struggle intensely with compliance to government requirements. That struggle includes the registration of their churches. Even Western relationships with Soviet Christians are largely controlled by debates about the legitimacy of the registered churches versus the unregistered underground church.

What's going on here? Is this a high moment for religion and democratic participation, or are we seeing the risk of the collapse of consensus government?

Civil disobedience in the context of religious liberty is an issue of critical importance in today's world. Those who disobey are real people who must struggle with the demands of the state versus the demands of their faith. There are thousands of them. I met seven I'll never forget: Pyotr, Augustina, Liliya, Lyuba, Lidia, Mariya, and Timothy. The "Siberian Seven" were members of two families, the Vashchenkos and the Chmykalovs, who lived for four years in a small basement room of the American embassy in Moscow as they sought release for themselves and their families.

In two visits to Moscow to seek their release, I sat with these simple folks—ate borsch, sang songs, prayed, laughed, cried. For years they had sought freedom to worship. Their political agendas were non-existent. They had no secret to share with the west. They were not famous scientists or writers, like Sakharov or Solzhenitsyn. But the system came down hard: there were prison terms, their children were removed from them, and they were harassed. The state said NO to their faith, to their worship, to their emigration. But they kept saying NO to the state with a tenacity and a faith I found appealing. They had never read a single volume on jurisprudence, hadn't heard of Thoreau, perhaps not even of King or Gandhi. But they knew there was an unshakeable claim on them. So they said NO to the great bear, to modern-day Russia.

# TWO

# What's Going On Here?

W HY HAVE INCREASING NUMBERS of Christians begun to speak of asserting their religious convictions in open confrontation with civil authorities? Why have people, unsuc-.cessful at persuading legislative bodies or judicial forums of the rightness of their cause, suddenly felt "called" or under some religious "duty" to engage in the dramatic activities evidenced in Bangor, Washington, and Louisville, Nebraska?

Surely, many complex social and personal elements are intermingled in any given instance of civil disobedience. Amateur and professional psychiatrists easily place such dissidents on their analytical couches to tell us what is going on. Yet, there are other elements which underlie the current rhetoric of confrontation. What we are witnessing is a religious phenomenon with theological elements interacting with other factors which also shape the current context.

### *Ambivalence*

Americans have had a long-term love-hate relationship with the law. On the one hand, we proudly declare ourselves to be a nation of law, not of men. Alexis de Tocqueville, in his visits to early America, noted our preoccupation with law and ob-served that lawyers were perhaps the "new American aristoc-racy." We have chosen law as the vehicle for much of our social change. In response to the celebration in the Marxist world of Communist values and hopes on May 1, we created Law Day.

Despite that, we are ambivalent about law. America's folklore, our entertainment, our films and television all show the other side. We have never been at all sure that law is adequate to the task of justice or that our legal institutions or personnel know the route to truth. Our frontier heritage with its glorification of the individual, suspicion of law, and preference for direct and informal, if noisy and messy, systems of justice are still with us. Lately, in the popular media, a sheriff is still likely to be portrayed as a bungling, ignorant, fat, and intimidated sycophant, or, alternatively, as a ruthless tyrant—not as a paragon of virtue or defender of justice. It is still often the private operator, the alien, the Lone Ranger who does justice. The non-system person ferrets out the guilty and hands them over to the system. Indeed, at times, they must overcome official apathy if not outright evil and corruption. The A-Team, pursued by malevolent law men, understands the truth, acts with integrity, and does justice. Their methods are more straightforward, their commitments more sure, their vision clearer than that of the bungling and stupid law-enforcers who are mired in regulations, self-interest, and resistance to outsiders.

## *Anger and Apocalypticism*

The rhetoric of both the religious left and right reveals an increasing level of frustration and anger with what is happening in our society. Christians of the right, who were generally satisfied to leave government to the politicians and who approved of such aphorisms as "religion and politics don't mix," have suddenly changed their minds. They see a nation that's lost its center and sold its birthright. They see a state, morally rudderless, a government that has mistakenly thought its sole task was to be the maximizing of individual liberty. George Will notes that the state has tragically forgotten its duty to the "soul."[1] Daniel Yankelovich declared that "the world is turned upside down" and likened the experience to an earthquake: "The giant plates of American culture are shifting relentlessly beneath us." He insisted, "We are not going back to the old way."

There is growing frustration at the loss of values in our society. Conservatives point to the explosion of pornography, the paralysis of our legal system in the face of growing crime, a drug culture which seems impenetrable, the collapse of the family, schools that are failures. But worse, the major institutions of our society are perceived as co-conspirators in the collapsing moral character of our nation. The media, television, and popular music glorify rebellion, ridicule traditional values of sexual fidelity and religious faith and foster violence. Our political leadership seems paralyzed. Our courts endorse abortion, squeeze religion out of public life, abuse their constitutional role, and are helpless in the face of crime because of their preoccupation with legal technicalities that avoid doing justice.

Further, having adopted the new values of secularism and "neutrality" as to any ideology, the state seeks to impose that valuelessness on the church. Virginia public authorites insisted that a realtor could not use a religious symbol on his stationery because that was "discrimination." Is the state, not content with its own lack of identity and, embarrassed by the notion of ideology itself, seeking to compel others to adopt its own confusion?

Many sense that, while the secularist speaks of neutrality, in fact, Christians are being excluded. H. Richard Niebuhr noted years ago the nature and expression of this hostility of secular culture to religion:

> The antagonism of modern, tolerant culture to Christ is of course often disguised because it does not call its religious practices religious, reserving the term for certain specified rites connected with officially recognized sacred institu-

tions; and also because it regards what it calls religion as one of many interests which can be placed alongside economics, art, science, politics and techniques. Hence the objection it voices to Christian monotheism appears in such injunctions only as that religions should be kept out of politics and business, or that Christians must learn to get along with other religions. *What is often meant is that not only the claims of religious groups but all consideration of the claims of Christ and God should be banished from the spheres where other gods, called values, reign.*[2] (emphasis supplied)

Other Christians, usually politically liberal, raise a different litany of tragedies: the arms race, proliferation of nuclear weapons, destruction of the environment, world hunger, violations of human rights, and immoral concentrations of power in multi-national corporations.

Whichever litany, there is an increased sense of confrontation between the ideology and interests of the state and the values and moral commitments of religious faith. The result is a sense of crisis, and the conviction that unless there is an impact of the Spirit, a sense of moral revival, a recovery of roots—our national ethos will collapse. Marches are held in Washington to call for national repentance. In a crisis, drastic action is demanded, perhaps heroic action. What is needed is prophetic action and witness—immune to intimidation, oblivious to claims of property, risking attack. It is time to sound the alarm, blow the trumpet, to call to battle.

Among the more extreme elements of Christian civil disobedience, this quickly leads to a sort of apocalypticism—a style of expression and action which sees the battle in cosmic terms, filled with urgency and ultimacy.

## The State

The very *character,* apart from its actions, of the modern state seems a substantial element in our openness to resistance.

Whether Orwellian fears of 1984 are exaggerated or not, there is a broad recognition and concern that the power of the modern state, combined with modern technology and the complexity of modern economic and political life, creates serious problems for individual liberty. Where shall privacy and humanity survive? Where is the space for conscience, for individuality?

It is not necessary to posit a malevolent state. In fact, the state that most genuinely seeks to do good may most threaten a genuine liberty and pluralism.

As the state involves itself increasingly in family life, economic regulations, environmental control, business regulation, and social legislation, there is both a political and a psychosocial concern for how the individual spirit can maintain vitality and freedom, given the complexity of modern government. Where are the structures and institutions which compete, ideologically and relationally, with the omnipresent state? Where are what Richard Neuhaus has called the "mediating structures?"

Government has swallowed up decision-making, and, no matter how benevolent, its imperialism and colonialism represents a serious threat not only to other centers of life (including the church and family) but also to the integrity of its own life. It now stands alone, unjudged and unchecked. William Ball, noted constitutional lawyer, has warned, "We are being overrun by a lava of government regulation, which, in every area of our lives, is becoming hardset." He likens our compliance to the attitudes one sees in Kafka of "the desire of the slave to exceed the Master's wishes."

### *Democratization—Power to the People?*

Perhaps as a reaction to the threat of powerful centralized life, not only in government but in media and economic life, there has been a trend symbolized by the populist cry, "Power to the People." It is an appeal to avoid losing control of our destiny. In one sense, there has been an increasing democratization of political life; grass roots organizations, local lobbying groups, special interests, and one-man-one-vote are some expressions of this groundswell. The demand is for a voice, the right to speak. There is an insistence on being heard, that government be responsive, that city "bosses" be thrown out and machines discarded.

But this may be as much a symbol of the loss of power as a claiming of it. It is doubtful that power-to-the-people slogans have much of an impact of the growing centralization of life. They do symbolize a frustration and a mood, a quest for control and relevance, which may easily create an environment for assertiveness in the political arena.

## Disillusionment

It further seems that we are seeing a collapse of a long-standing common ethos in American public life, what some have called (probably a little too optimistically) the Judeo-Christian heritage. Whatever the source or basis of this common culture, it created a comfortable sense of mutuality between the interests of the state and those of much of religion. To be sure, there have always been elements in American society which did not participate in this ethos. Initially, few religious groups were included, but even in a much broader sense of definition, many still were left out. The outsiders were often called "cults" if their views were perceived as really bizarre, "sects" if they were merely seen as quaint, such as the Amish. But most religious persons saw few conflicts between their aspirations and those of American society at large. Law, for them, expressed many of these commitments. It was a partnership, or at least an alliance, between church and state, and among her peoples. There was no need for a prophet to insist, "Choose ye this day whom ye shall serve." Leading politicians were (or at least wanted us to believe they were) churchmen. Piety, as long as it wasn't extreme, was no liability to political success.

The courts acknowledged this state of affairs in language such as Justice Douglas' in *Zorach* v. *Clausen* : "We are a religious people whose institutions presuppose the existence of a Supreme Being." Constitutional principles of "accommodation" and "benevolent neutrality" kept the First Amendment ban on the "establishment of religion" from creating hostility toward religion. The concept of the separation of church and state, in part, held its vitality because of a certain kind of symbiotic relationship between church and state. They could be separate spheres because to a large extent they were non-competing spheres. The same basic moral, and often religious, commitments motivated each. The symbols of this comfortable relationship are many—the language on our coins, Washington prayer breakfasts, Thanksgiving proclamations, government chaplains, and so on.

That partnership, as perceived by more and more religious persons, has collapsed. It is now clear that increasing numbers of Christians are either convinced that that relationship was always an unholy alliance or that the relationship has been broken by government abandonment of these common moral principles. In either case, on both the religious left and the right, there is an increased sense of confrontation and distance. For many, it is a sense of disillusionment with government. The continued church-state battles in the courts are more a sign of frustration with the lost consensus than they are a real battle over the shape of the alliance.

This disillusionment actually extends beyond the issue of religion and the state. More centrally, the issue is one of identification with America, and more explicitly, identification with its laws and political institutions. In much of our history, Christians shared and even led their fellow citizens in a rousing tribute to, almost a worship of, America. America was, after all, the new Israel, the hope of the world, the preserver of democracy. We were, in the main, a good and righteous people. Founded by Christians seeking freedom of worship (at least for themselves), declaring at the outset that our liberty was rooted in God, it was difficult to approve of disobedience to a government which seemed so directly to be an instrument of God's work for justice and liberty in the world. Christians easily placed the American flag beside the Christian flag in their churches and were both confused and angry that religious groups like the Jehovah's Witnesses might decline to salute the flag and dare to call the government demonic.

In recent years, the sense of America as God's chosen people has been repeatedly challenged. To be sure it has been challenged ideologically by a more proper biblical sense of the judgment of God over all nations. More significantly, however, has been an increased awareness of the evil that has lurked in our own history. As our consciousness has been quickened about the issue of civil rights, treatment of the American Indians, self-interest evident in our foreign policy, and "dirty politics," it has been less and less clear that America stood arm and arm with God. Watergate, with its repeated stories of judicial and legislative corruption, has made sharply clear that the worship of America's political and economic systems has been a tragic mistake.

Now, with the mantle of righteousness shorn from political and social life, it is more appropriate to find oneself out of touch, out of tune, and in confrontation with that society. Christians are sensing that they are a minority people with an alien citizenship. The prevailing culture, or at least its makers and shapers, concur that religionists are curious cultural artifacts. We are all now Amish. Sociologically, more and more religionists are seen as "cultic," out of sync with "public policy." This situation involves something of an identity crisis for believers, a kind of coming of age, a rite of passage.

## The Relativization of Law

Western man is undergoing an integrity crisis. . . . Our whole culture seems to be facing the possibility of a kind of nervous breakdown. . . . One major symptom of this threatened breakdown is the massive loss of confidence in the law.

Harold Berman
Story Professor of Law, Harvard Law School

The law itself is in crisis as to its nature, character, and source. This crisis is a substantial, though largely unrecognized, aspect of the emergence of civil disobedience today. Our very understanding of law has changed. This shift has had a significant impact on the degree to which civil disobedience seems appropriate.

The nature of law is critical to our consideration of civil disobedience in a number of respects. When one disobeys the law, what is it that is being challenged? What is "law" and its claim upon us? Our perception of the nature of law and its source may also affect our sense of the likely consequences to law of a refusal to follow it on grounds of a higher law. Our jurisprudence does affect our obedience!

From ancient Greek philosophy through western Christendom, the persistent conviction has been that law and religion were closely intertwined, and that law, to be valid, must express the will of God. Demosthenes had declared that "every law is a discovery and gift of God." Law which failed to be in accord with the law of God, the natural law, was in fact, not law. Augustine echoed that understanding. William Blackstone, whose law books formed the educational curriculum for early American lawyers, summed it up: "The law of nature . . . dictated by God himself . . . is binding in all countries at all times; no human laws are of any validity if contrary to this."

While such a notion is one of the bases for establishing the legitimacy of civil disobedience, the actual effect through much of our history has been to give law a sanction, an authority that discouraged disobedience. When law is perceived as the sovereign expression of divine law, as some earthly manifestation, however limited, of some higher law, it is only at great risk that one chooses to disobey. Law is not just law, but LAW.

American law stood largely within that tradition, but, even as the mythology of the state has been largely shattered, so has this image of the law. While many Christians might yearn for the day when law expressed some approximation of God's law or natural justice, there is an increased recognition that law today is to a degree a product of political lobbying, self-interest, and the general socio-political process.

Harold Berman suggests that only four of ten basic presuppositions or characteristics of Western law remain valid today—a change he views with alarm. He notes that law is no longer a "coherent whole" but rather a "fragmented mass of ad-hoc decisions" with a resultant replacement of a high vision of law with a "kind of cynicism." Law is no longer perceived as it once was as transcending politics and distinct from the state but now as rather "basically an instrumentality of the state." He concludes:

> The crisis of the Western legal tradition is not merely a crisis in legal philosophy, but a crisis in law itself. . . . As a matter of historical fact, the legal system of all the nations that are heirs to the Western legal tradition have been rooted in certain beliefs and postulates. Today those beliefs or postulates—such as the structural integrity of law, its ongoingness, its religious roots, its transcendant qualities—are rapidly disappearing, not only from the minds of lawmakers, judges, lawyers, law teachers, and other members of the legal profession, but from the conciousness of the vast majority of citizens. . . . The law is becoming more fragmented, more subjective, geared more to expediency and less to morality, concerned more with immediate consequences and less with consistency or continuity. Thus the historical soil of the Western legal tradition is being washed away in the twentieth century.[3]

The natural law tradition has been largely replaced by positivist and sociological views of jurisprudence, notions that law is simply the product of a social and political process. Law, as a leading philosopher of law insisted, is merely "a command with a sanction." It reflects not truth or justice, but power. As noted legal scholar John Chipman Gray insisted, lawyers don't discover law, they "are the creators of law." Law is thus evolutionary, tentative, experimental. This relativism in the law has enormous consequences for society.

Jacques Ellul, in his *Theological Foundation of Law*, notes four consequences of the abolition of a concept of natural law:

1. Law ceases to be measured against any concept of justice and becomes "purely a combination of technical rules . . . a mere skill."

2. Judicial technique is at the disposal of whoever wishes to take advantage of it. The "technique is manipulated according to new and arbitrary criteria, substituted for ideas of justice and natural law. . . . Agglomeration of rules and regulations has no longer anything to do with law. It is meant to favor the power of the strong who, in turn, justifies his position by endowing the juridical system with the new criteria, 'law.'"

3. The capacity for law to limit and inhibit the state is destroyed. "The state has a free hand . . . No longer is the state judged in its actions by the law."

4. The law gradually ceases to be observed and respected. "The affinity between man and law is gone . . . it strikes no truly responsive chord in man. . . . Man no longer sees why he should obey this law. Law is molded according to economic and political necessities and becomes absurd . . . man in the street no longer acknowledges it as authentic."[4]

If law is largely a product of social and political processes, then several inferences may be drawn for the issue of civil disobedience. First, one may decide that if law is hammered out on the anvil of socio-political process, including political and economic pressure, then one had better be involved in that process—boycotts, demonstrations, confrontations, and political threat.

Second, existing law would seem to lose much of its divine sanction, at least as to *content,* because there is little reason to believe that it represents any sense of ultimacy. Why, after all, should we grant any ultimate authority to yesterday's power and political persuasion, or to what a positivist may view as little more than "a command with a sanction"? Such laws are more a part of the world which is passing away, a world to which we ought not conform, as men of today, let alone as men of God.

Third, since one's biblical duty is to do justice (which is an ethical concept) and not law (since law, by definition, is now a political category and not an ethical or moral one), one *may* conclude that one is free, at least as to ethics, to disregard the law. If no one pretends law is accountable to justice for its content and validity, then why should we feel compelled to grant it the obeisance we would give to an approximation of justice?

Fourth, for some, even the word *law* may no longer be an appropriate term for such a sociological "accident," any more than *truth* is a proper term for Orwellian magistrates, or *equality* for the politics at *Animal Farm.* Following Augustine and Aquinas, one might conclude that not much "law" exists anymore, though the number of social rules and punishable acts or omissions decreed by the state may be numerous. In a theoretical sense, an Augustinian could argue that one was not even engaged in civil disobedience if one was simply ignoring positivist "law" since it was not really law unless it conformed to LAW.

Thus initially, it would seem that a positivist conception of law ought to be more open to law resistance (since law is flexible and evolutionary), in fact, positivism has not only kicked the props out from under law, but from higher-law-based civil disobedience. The positivist frequently belittles talk of justice and truth. If there is no higher law, then on what basis may I insist that law is immoral or unethical? To what may I point to show the inadequacy and injustice of law? Since law's authority is no longer viewed as its *justice,* but simply its *existence,* then I am constrained to silence.

It is not chiefly civil disobedience which brings disrespect to the law. The demeaning of the legal order by its loss of reference to something beyond itself invites avoidance and even contempt.

## A God of History

While political aspects of contemporary society, the sociology of our relationship to law, and our jurisprudence doubtless impact our readiness for civil disobedience, perhaps even more significant is the religious element.

Participants root their civil disobedience in religious commitments. From the fringe element like Gordon Kahl and Posse Comitatus to nationally revered figures such as Martin Luther King, the language is one of duty to God. Not infrequently acts of civil disobedience are even accompanied by prayers, singing of hymns, and religious liturgy. Disobedients speak of being "led by the spirit" and describe their experiences almost in conversion language. Jim Douglas, leader of demonstrations at the Trident base, described what happened as they reached the first nuclear bunker: "We stood in silence for several minutes on the concrete entry, joined hands, and said aloud the Lord's Prayer and the Hail Mary." Molly Rush, arrested in another nuclear protest, recounted her gradual acceptance of her willingness to risk civil disobedience: "As I let go of my trust in myself and began to trust more in God, fears that earlier immobilized me faded away."

But the more significant religious element is not the religious emotions and language, but the theological commitment inherent in civil protests. This commitment represents, for conservative elements, a dramatic shift with enormous implications for religion in American life. In one sense, the most striking thing is not the *content* or focus of the opposition, but the *fact* of it.

In earlier days in America, Christians of all persuasions, including evangelical Protestants, took active roles in speaking out on public issues. Religious leadership was predominant in the anti-slavery movements. However, evangelicalism was soon dominated by pietistic and revivalist traditions. Religious bodies which developed in the frontiers of American society, primarily Baptists and Methodists, emphasized an exclusively other-worldly religion of personal holiness and salvation. These perspectives have dominated much of American evangelical Protestantism since the Civil War.

Fundamentalists became even more withdrawn from public and urban affairs in reaction to the vigorous engagement by liberal Protestants in what was called the "social gospel." Fundamentalists not only saw little religious meaning in politics and no salvation in culture, but they were, in fact, quite hostile to any such engagement. Roger Williams' image of the garden and wilderness gained new currency; the wilderness (the state) must not be allowed in the garden (the church), lest the garden lose its purity and beauty. This avoidance of responsibility for the character of public life was further encouraged by an eschatological view which saw the imminent return of Christ to take believers out of the world and judge what was left. The institutions of this world were unworthy of attention in the face of the urgent tasks of preparation for his coming. Separation, avoidance of worldliness, and moral purity were the hallmarks of this tradition. This world was passing away, and the task of the believer was to prepare for the next. Maintaining purity of heart and winning others to the kingdom was the primary task of the believer. Public affairs could hardly compete with such priorities.

Even the American notions of separation of church and state, and popular aphorisms like "Don't mix religion and politics" confirmed a way of looking at religion that encouraged the privatization of religion and compartmentalization of life. These perspectives became the mainstream evangelical hallmark. While alternatives, particularly in the Reformed and Catholic traditions, continued to speak of the Christian faith's relevance for public affairs, they captured very little of the American enthusiasm for religion.

In recent years, however, something of a theological revival has occurred among those traditionally content to let the world go by. This revival has essentially been a recovery of central biblical themes about the kingdom of God, the Lordship of Christ, redemption, and creation. As evangelicals and conservatives have rethought the implications of the Lordship of Jesus Christ and the doctrine of creation, the relevance of the gospel for arenas of life beyond worship and evangelism has become clear. The notion of incarnation itself implies an engagement with materiality and history. The Judeo-Christian scriptures saw God acting in the processes of history, in the anointing of kings, in the doing of justice at the gate, in the making and avoiding of military alliances. As a God of history, God's character and judgment occur in "real time." History not only carries within it the story of God's acts, but it is the raw material out of which genuine religious life is woven. There is no escape to "religion" for a biblical people. Faith is not so much an escape from the world and its ambiguities, as an insertion into it as agents of reconciliation and blessing. The "called out" ones are returned as witnesses and signs.

Prophetic religion speaks to the state about justice, the duties of kings, economic righteousness, and public duties. Nations are called to create structures and institutions which do justice and show mercy.

With such a biblical commitment, the people of God cannot avoid cultural responsibility. They must be a witness to all creation. They are stewards of all the earth. Religion may not be seen as an escape from the world, the creation of a private zone, the adoption of a cultic liturgy, and a heavenly God. Rather, in proclaiming a Lord of all creation, Christian faith is, as William Temple insisted, the most worldly of all religions.

Similarly, concepts of community and culture become relevant in this newly claimed theology. A community built around a covenant and a law can hardly ignore the processes by which God has developed his people and created a body.

Now it is clear that religion and politics must mix. Church and state may be separate, but religion and the state dare not be. Religion, touching all of life, must touch our whole approach to life—relationships, justice, education.

So contrary to our national experience is such interaction that when Moral Majority leader Jerry Falwell began to speak out of his religious understanding on public issues, a hue and cry was raised by secularists who condemned such "interference" and "meddling" as contrary to American constitutional thought, divisive, and wholly inappropriate. Even liberal church leaders who themselves had spoken out on public issues suddenly wanted Falwell to be quiet and stick to "religion."

But, with a full orbed commitment to a biblical perspective, sticking to "religion" was precisely what could no longer happen. Christians of the right had come out of the closet. Critics had complained they were so heavenly-minded that they were no earthly good, that they were escapist, privatistic. A good many of them aren't any more, but they still aren't loved!

Just as Christians were developing an ideology requiring engagement with the world and participation in its affairs, the culture was increasingly moving toward discounting religion and insisting it stay in its place. Closets were the place for prayer and churches for religion, the secularist insisted, with the conviction he was expressing great theology as well as political tolerance.

## *Athens to Louisville, Where Now?*

It is with this "baggage" and these commitments, that the issue of civil disobedience is thrust before the Christian community and the individual believer. The issue of civil disobedience is hardly new. The dilemma created by a conflict between one's sense of duty, or conscience, and one's place in the community and duty to society, or the state, is a classic confrontation. Even Lady Godiva's daring ride was a tax protest. The clash is not only at the political level but in the inner psyche as well, and, at both the political and personal level, the elements of religious faith and conviction impinge. Martin Luther King and Gandhi did not create the issue, nor were they the first to seek to resolve it.

It is the struggle faced by Sophocles' *Antigone,* torn between her personal sense of filial obligations and the law. Antigone, forbidden by King Creon to bury the corpse of her brother, is convinced of the injustice of Creon's order, both under divine law and custom, and chooses to bury her brother secretly. She is condemned to death but takes her own life.

It is the same struggle Socrates faced when convicted of impiety and of corrupting youth. He insists that there is a duty owed to the state, which bars him from seeking to escape punishment. "You must do whatever your city or your country bid you to do, or you must convince them that their commands are unjust." Yet he cannot conform to the demands of the state because he has a duty to a higher law:

Men of Athens, I honor and love you; but I shall obey God rather than you, and while I have life and strength I shall never cease from the practice and teaching of my philosophy . . . either acquit me or not; but whichever you do, understand that I shall never alter my ways, not even if I have to die many times.[5]

The issues today are urgent ones, not because they are new, nor simply because some resolution must be forthcoming in the specific instances of civil disobedience which are acted out in modern society. The issues are urgent because behind them rest fundamental questions about our society, the role of the State, the proper means of moral discourse in our society, the meaning of conscience, and the balancing of the demands which rest upon us as individuals, believers, and citizens. At root, the issues of civil disobedience are basic philosophic, jurisprudential, and theological questions.

But, at another level, for Christians, they are issues of the duties of discipleship. The issues are those of biblical principles, the guidance of the Holy Spirit, the exercise of discernment, and the resolution of the conflicts between obedience and witness. For the believer, the legal and general philosophic debates will take backseat to the questions of God's will for Christian faithfulness.

The scope of the issues, and their tenacious complexity, should dissolve any expectation that this volume will either be exhaustive or definitive. The purpose is to assist in exploring the issues, examining the nature of biblical and Christian thinking (albeit in a necessarily summary fashion), and suggesting some fundamental concepts and prudential principles for Christians who are increasingly sensitive to the claims of God clashing with those of contemporary culture. To not be conformed to this world is the clear command of scripture, but what shall it mean for us in relationship to our public life?

The issues will not go away. Peculiar people and aliens living in a strange land will normally encounter many Nebuchadnezzars and Caesars with their idols and ideologies. At times, minorities may benignly give consent by silence, at other times by service, and, tragically, at times by worship.

The modern State is likely to be more sophisticated in its terminology and methodology. If Marxist, its power may be narrowly centralized and overt, with tools of oppression and exclusion. If democratic, its power will appear diffused and baptized with "consent." It will speak of public policy, pluralism, the will of the people, the common good. Its tools are more likely to be licenses, grants, exemptions, offices, seats of honor. But its capacity for oppression, for being a "principality" and a "power," is not less clear.

In the face of all this, we must act in consistency with our evangelical proclamation that Jesus Christ is Lord!

# THREE

# Definitions: A Rose by Any Other Name . . .

O UR DEFINITIONS FOR CIVIL DISOBEDIENCE will, to a large extent, affect our evaluations of it.

The term itself is somewhat ambiguous, having been described by one philosopher as an "open concept" and by another as "vague." In America in particular, the term has been largely defined, not in the abstract, but by reference to those who have most contributed to its moral approbations: Mahatma Gandhi and Martin Luther King. It is difficult to conceive of the notion of civil disobedience without special attention being given to the way in which they understood its character and practice. Yet even with these models, problems of meaning remain.

Part of the definitional problem stems from the wide range of conduct which has been labeled civil disobedience. Daniel Berrigan pouring napalm over draft records, looters and rioters in Newark, Rosa Parks refusing to move to the back of the bus, Indians making salt in violation of the law, civil rights protestors engaging in sit-ins at restaurants, Siberian Pentecostals refusing to perform military service, Church of the Brethren professors making symbolic deductions from tax forms, John Brown at Harpers Ferry: all these were described by participants or observers as acts of civil disobedience. They all violated the law—but their motives, purposes, and forms are so radically diverse that one wonders if a single term like civil disobedience can encompass such diversity.

## Motives

Definitions are also difficult because of the varied *motives* of persons who conscientiously break laws. Some act out of a conviction that the law resisted is unconstitutional; others, that the law is immoral. Yet others hold that by cooperating with a law they are enabling conditions necessary for some other offensive policy to be enforced, or that the law, however just in the abstract, is unjust in a particular case, or that the law is unjust to those not in a position to protest for themselves.

## Purposes

Not only may motives be varied but the *purposes* of disobedience vary widely. The purposes of non-compliance include avoidance of doing wrong, calling attention to an injustice, interfering with the operation or implementation of a proposed law, awakening the public to an evil, slowing or halting the operation of the law, disrupting some structured order for the purpose of forcing changes in the social structure, or, even more radically, undermining the authority of government officials. Given this diversity, it is essential to establish in what sense we are using the term civil disobedience so that any judgments or affirmations of it will be made within a common context.

## Characteristics of Civil Disobedience

In much of the literature regarding the definition or characteristics of civil disobedience, it is often unclear whether the factors or criteria suggested are definitional or evaluative. Have those qualities been selected primarily to give clarity and precision to the term, or have they also been selected, at least in part, with a view to affecting our moral judgment about the conduct? At least some of the qualities noted below are attempts to confine civil disobedience to those characteristics which distinguish it from revolution and which preserve its moral integrity.

Morris Keeton defines civil disobedience as "an act of deliberate and open violation of the law with the intent, within the prevailing framework of government, to protest a wrong or to accomplish some betterment in the society."[1] Noted legal philosopher John Rawls seems to identify the same notions when he describes civil disobedience as a public, nonviolent, and conscientious act, contrary to law, usually done with the intent to bring about a change in the policies or laws of the government.

The chief elements which are embodied in these sample definitions reflect a common understanding of civil disobedience:

**1. The Breaking of the Law.** Not all law-breaking is civil disobedience. Ma Barker and Jesse James may have become folk heroes—but they were not engaged in civil disobedience. Even Robin Hood, who robs with the allegedly noble purpose of redistributing wealth, is not engaged in civil disobedience. Irish, Israeli, or Palestinian terrorists would only under the most exaggerated notions of the term be perceived as engaging in civil disobedience.

Not all acts of protest or attempts to change society involve the breaking of the law. We are not discussing breaking a social convention or conduct in poor taste, but conduct in violation of the law.

At times, civil disobedience has been used to describe all kinds of unpopular dissent. Thus, protest marches, demonstrations, and other conduct which is socially disruptive and offensive to those who support the protested law or policies are described as acts of civil disobedience. In fact, there is often nothing "disobedient" about them at all. Most forms of dissent are not illegal; they are clearly within established legal rights. Even some conduct which may appear outside the legal norms may be protected by the free exercise clause, or statutorily protected, such as conscientious objector status.

Law-breaking conduct may involve either commission or omission; that is, it may be either positive or negative, active or passive. One may positively and actively commit acts prohibited by the law, such as operating a school in violation of a court order, sitting in a prohibited portion of a bus, or holding a demonstration in a prohibited area like the Capitol rotunda. Alternatively, one may passively refuse to take some action required and mandated by law, such as serving in the military, paying taxes, registering one's school, or carrying a draft card.

It is also important to distinguish civil disobedience from revolution. Civil disobedience is law-breaking, not government-breaking. To some extent, civil disobedience may be related to the possible justifications for revolution. In that sense, it is on the same legal continuum as revolution. The overwhelming consensus, however, is that civil disobedience ought to be distinguished from revolutionary and anarchistic philosophies and movements. This in spite of the fact that Thoreau, one of the most influential shapers of civil disobedience thought, tended to anarchism and that Gandhi, the person whose conduct has most shaped the concept, had an ultimate revolutionary component to his thinking. Gandhi intended the replacement of the British government in India, not its mere improvement.

Yet it seems more proper to confine the use of the term "civil disobedience" to contexts where the resister accepts the legitimacy of the existing government and affirms the general legal order. Carl Cohen acknowledges that civil disobedience may lead to a revolutionary conspiracy, but that civil disobedience as such "acts *within* the frame of established authority not outside of it."

Maintaining the distinction between civil disobedience and

political rebellion is not an issue of mere etymology. Much recent civil disobedience in the United States has dealt primarily with appeals to the community and the legal process within the existing political structure. It has not been an attempt to supplant it. While the Stokely Carmichaels and Rap Browns talked in a revolutionary idiom, the vast majority who fought for civil rights simply called on the existing government and its processes to reflect higher moral values and a more noble vision. They did not primarily claim that the government was illegitimate, but that it had failed to do justice in a specific area. The "dream" was not apocalyptic.

It is also quite legitimate to expect that rebellion and revolution require a much greater degree, if not kind, of justification than conscientious acts of civil disobedience. Threats to the entire social and political order and the security of society are clearly more serious than challenges to specific acts of a government or its impositions on the personal level. Confining civil disobedience to the latter assists in avoiding the problem of criticizing such conscientious acts on false assumptions that the acts are antinomian or anarchistic.

Lewis Feuer, then professor of sociology at the University of Toronto, affirmed and summed up the distinction between civil disobedience and civil resistance:

> The first is limited to dramatizing a particular issue, it retains a faith in representative democracy, and takes for granted that once the facts are known and the people sense a responsibility awaken, the necessary reforms will be made. ... [Civil resistance, on the contrary, is] total and unlimited, for a claim the entire society is corrupt. ... It regards each episode as part of a guerilla warfare against society. It twists the vocabulary of civil disobedience to this purpose.[2]

**2. Conscientiously Initiated.** The second element in civil disobedience is that the law-breaking must be based on some moral conviction. It is the raising of a moral claim that creates the essential tension about the legitimacy of civil disobedience. It creates the debate first about the correctness of the claim of a higher, moral duty; and second, the argument about whether that moral duty legitimizes the law-breaking that is at the heart of the debate about civil disobedience.

The act must be conscientious in the sense that the individual realizes the legitimacy of law itself and "proposes to justify his disobedience by an appeal to the incompatibility between his political circumstances and his moral convictions." For the actor, it is worse to obey than to disobey it.[3]

To indicate that the law-breaking has been based on conscience, is not, in and of itself, a justification. Conscience may be wrong, or even if correct, an insufficient warrant for disobedience. This issue we shall address later; here we are concerned not with objective morality, but with subjective.

These two elements, the *law-breaking* and the *conscience* principles are at the core of civil disobedience. However, as noted in the definitions above, there is a tendency to go beyond these two elements and further refine the concept, usually by the inclusion of the following traditional elements.

**3. Public in Character.** Martin Luther King in his "Letter from a Birmingham Jail" wrote, "one who breaks an unjust law must do so openly, lovingly, and with a willingness to accept the penalty."[4]

The very character of civil disobedience as moral witness requires it to be public, not secret, law-breaking. There may, occasionally, even be advance notice of the disobedient act. Hugo Bedau has noted, however, another sense in which the acts are public: "The dissenter views what he does as a civic act, an act that properly belongs to the public life of the community . . . his act draws attention to something he thinks the whole community should be brought to consider, since the community has as much interest in the act as he does."[5] The violator is not attempting to hide from the authorities either *who* is engaged in the act, or the *nature* of the act being committed. When there is an attempt to hide, the acts more properly are an evasion of the law and not civil disobedience.

This concept of the public character of the acts is not without exception. The Underground Railroad is generally understood to have been civil disobedience. The consequences of being *public*, not only to the facilitators but to their clients, provided clear cause for avoiding the public dimension. The acts were certainly protests against the law, and conscience-based, though not public. It is more important to see this as an exception rather than as requiring a new category.

**4. Willing Acceptance of Punishment.** "Under a government which imprisons any unjustly, the true place for a just man is also a prison," declared Thoreau. Perhaps these words of Thoreau are the basis of the (probably spurious) story that when Emerson visited Thoreau in jail and inquired what his friend "was doing in there?" Thoreau replied, "What are you doing out there?"

It is commonly suggested that for an act to be properly in the purview of civil disobedience, the actor must be willing to accept the punishment meted out by the law for the acts committed. To some extent this is a corollary of the "public character" of the act. Roger Baldwin, first president of the American Civil Liberties Union, was arrested for failing to register for the draft in the First World War. In a letter to the New York Attorney General, he explained his views and indicated he would not seek to avoid the penalties: "I do not seek martyrdom. I desire no public notoriety. . . . All I ask of you is a speedy trial. I shall, of course, plead guilty."

The willingness to accept punishment is, for many religious dissenters, an aspect of "submission" to authority, which is perceived as a critical dimension of biblical command. Thus a distinction is often drawn by Christian war resisters between those "draft-dodgers" who publicly opposed the draft and accepted the punishment, and those who sought to evade the law by fleeing the jurisdiction.

More recent non-religious literature about civil disobedience shows some "slippage" in the principle of voluntary acceptance of punishment. Modern protesters at the march on the Pentagon in Washington or demonstrators protesting Dow Chemical Company's manufacture of napalm did not willingly accept punishment, much less plead guilty. Daniel Berrigan jumped bail after his conviction.

Howard Zinn, in *Conscience and Democracy*, attacks an alleged "fallacy" that the person who commits civil disobedience must accept the punishment. For Zinn, if the law is grossly unjust, any punishment for deliberately breaking it is itself unjust and the disobedient need not accept such punishment.[6] Such an argument seems to ignore any independent moral duty to obey the law itself. As Carl Cohen notes, "accepting the punishment when one has deliberately broken a good law is the only way to show . . . respect. To evade the punishment, therefore, is to emasculate the protest."[7]

Zinn expresses the more radical challenge to the notion of willing acceptance of punishment when he declares:

> If a social function of protest is to change the unjust condition of society, then that protest cannot stop with a court decision or jail sentence. If the protest is morally justified, it is morally justified to the very end, even past the point where a court has imposed a penalty. If it stops at that point, with everyone saying cheerfully, as at a football match "Well, we played a good game, we lost, and we will accept the verdict like good sports"—then we are treating social protest as a game. It becomes a token, a gesture. How potent an effect can protest have if it stops dead in its tracks as soon as the very government it is criticizing, decides against it?[8]

**5. Nonviolent in Character.** Both Gandhi and King insist that civil disobedience be nonviolent, even loving. Most philosophers of civil disobedience find the adjective "loving" a bit too much.

While the use of the term *civil* in civil disobedience properly refers to the fact that the disobedience involves orders of civil authorities (and does not refer to the issue of whether it is the civil or the criminal law which is violated), there is an aspect of civility involved. Acts of deliberate injury to persons or property, riot, and sabotage are not civil disobedience. Cohen notes: "Of course, a civil protest may be greeted most uncivilly, but as long as the protester does not respond in kind his conduct may remain civil. This means he must be prepared to meet violence with nonviolence and suffer the consequences. ... It is surely clear that civil disobedience is not child's play."[9]

Weingartner declares: "Civil disobedience must be *civil* disobedience of the law. If those who disobey the law use violence in doing so they are no longer practicing civil disobedience. . . . Instead, it becomes a defiance of the authority that makes and enforces the law. Violent disobedience is not simply a noisier kind of civil disobedience; it is rebellion."[10]

Nonviolence is a central element of civil disobedience, then, because it is consistent with the basic objectives of a legal system—the security of persons and property—whereas violent disobedience fails in this regard and threatens the very character of a community.

There are further historical reasons for the insistence that civil disobedience be nonviolent. For both Gandhi and Martin Luther King, nonviolence was not simply a tactic, but a central way of life. There are a number of problems, however, with the concept and requirement of nonviolence. To what extent should the notion of nonviolence be extended to cover the predictable reactions of those against whom one is protesting, or the society in general? Is it sufficient to be personally nonviolent when one knows that one's act is likely to excite violence? Or what about actions which, though nonviolent in a physical sense, nevertheless, are intended to or will have consequences so embarrassing or humiliating to persons as to fill them with hatred? What about violence to property? At least in their higher moments, both Gandhi and

King rejected any acts of violence or even intimidation, since their goal was not simply to win the struggle but rather to convert the opponent.

Normally, however, nonviolence refers to physical violence and not to the emotional, psychic, or social pressures which civil disobedience may engender.

Recent writers, ranging from the Marxist Herbert Marcuse to theologian Reinhold Niebuhr, have taken exception to the categorical elimination of violence from the concept of civil disobedience. Niebuhr suggests that the conclusion of ethicists that civil disobedience must necessarily be nonviolent emerges from two logical errors. The first is the misconception that violence must always be an expression of evil, and nonviolence, of good will; and the second, the confusion of instrumental values, such as peacefulness, with ultimate values.

## Summary

While there are obvious differences of perspective regarding precise elements required for civil disobedience, the majority of observers require several components for civil disobedience: law violation which is morally based; violation which is public in character; violation which is essentially nonviolent; and the willingness on the part of the law-breaker to accept the consequences of his conduct by willing acceptance of punishment.

## Types of Civil Disobedience

In addition to issues of definitions it is important, and often central to moral evaluation, to note the various *types* of civil disobedience. One mode of distinction may be based on the general *motive* of the actor. Two basic types of motives are evident.

One is illustrated by the actor whose personal conscience is indeed quickened, but whose basic motivation is not so much personal as it is public: the purpose is to initiate social or political change. Notions of justice and equity are predominant. Civil disobedience is usually instrumental, a means to an end. To be left alone or ignored would constitute defeat. The action is a *tactic*, largely intended to draw attention to unjust law, to embarrass leadership in the face of immoral law or government practice, or to rally public opinion. It must emerge out of a moral concern and reflect more than simply preferred political views, but it is political in the fullest sense of that term.

Alternatively there are also those persons whose acts of conscientious disobedience are not motivated primarily, or even at all, by an attempt to change the law or to compel civil authorities to adjust government policy. Rather, they are privately disobedient. Their conscience will not permit them to abide by the law. It is not a sense of justice that prods their conscience, but a sense of personal right or purity or integrity. They seek to act consistently with their moral or religious convictions and often simply wish to be left alone. To be ignored is victory. They say no to government, but make no demands of government. Thus the operator of a private Christian school may not object to laws about registering schools, but only wish to be exempt from that government policy.

The latter category is illustrated by Emerson's reported comment on reading the fugitive slave law of 1850: "By God, I will not obey it." Dr. Gene Sharp described those who wish to remain true to their own moral convictions, but are not attempting to persuade others to change law or policy, as "non-resistant," and notes that various Christian groups, such as Mennonite and Amish, fall into this category.

They pay their taxes, however, and do what the state demands, as long as it is not inconsistent with what they consider to be their duty to God. They refuse to resist evil situations even by non-violent techniques, and in times of oppression, simply hold to their beliefs and follow them — ignoring the evil as much as possible, and suffering their lot as part of their religious duty. But non-resistants are concerned with being true to their beliefs and maintaining their own integrity, rather than with attempts at social reconstruction, many even opposing attempts to create a good society here on earth.[11]

So distinctive are these two types of civil disobedience, that some analysts have suggested that the conscientious-exemptions type, should not even properly be called civil disobedience. They contend that civil disobedience must involve a protest. They would eliminate from "civil disobedience" those acts which are not part of some kind of public political protest. They label these more private acts as conscientious disobedience or non-cooperation.

The exclusion of such persons from the definition of civil disobedience is largely unwarranted. Even given the notion of protest, "a man who states or shows publicly that he believes a law or government policy offends morality, and that he is willing to go to jail rather than to obey or cooperate, has protested, whether he seeks by that act to get the law or policy changed or merely wishes to make his own moral position known."[12]

For many within a Christian tradition of civil disobedience, it is the latter form that has the most appeal and legitimacy. It is also the latter form which by its nature is almost always nonviolent, and tends to be intensely private. One of the problems of the political-protest type of civil disobedience is that it often involves group action. In the context of the group, issues of conscientiousness and even of nonviolence become more difficult to identify and manage, as Gandhi discovered in applying principles of nonviolence to mass demonstrations.

The second important mode of distinction is that between *direct* and *indirect* civil disobedience. In direct civil disobedience, the law disobeyed is the law which is morally objectionable. Thus, one who refuses to register for the draft or refuses to seek a permit for a day-care center is disobeying the very law which is opposed. Direct civil disobedience is the more traditional form and is usually the easiest to justify. We understand, even if we do not agree, why the particular law was ignored. Virtually all non-political, conscientious civil disobedience is *direct*.

Frequently, and more commonly of late, civil disobedience has involved the violation of laws not in and of themselves objectionable. The law is violated as a means of calling attention to some other objectionable law. In the civil rights movement, for example, it was quite common for the actual laws violated to be trespass laws. The civilly disobedient did not generally object to trespass laws, but their sit-ins were intended to call attention to another kind of wrong: racial segregation. Similarly, the acts of persons breaking into secured military areas to engage in their "stations of the cross" do not object to laws that bar the cutting of fences but object to military policies.

At times, the selection of laws to be disobeyed, not themselves objectionable, is necessary because one cannot disobey the law objected to. It is, for example, impossible to disobey a non-existent law. If one opposes the lack of laws regarding the killing of whales or the lack of laws regarding abortion or pornography, it is not possible to disobey those non-existing laws. At other times, what is objectionable are policies which are also inaccessible, e.g., policies regarding nuclear weapons, promotion of sexual permissiveness in television, and so on. In such instances, once one makes a commitment to engage in civil disobedience as a means of protest, to raise public consciousness, or to "witness," the only disobedience available is to select other laws. At times, the laws disobeyed may have a close relationship, at least symbolically, to the morally objectionable law or policy. At other times, it appears the law chosen to be violated is selected more on the basis of public visibility, newsworthiness, or the less worthy objectives of substantial disruption of the functioning of government. Breaking into a nuclear weapons base, spilling blood on draft records, or tearing up draft cards are more closely related to the objectionable government policies than would be true, for example, of holding a sit-in at the Capitol rotunda or blocking traffic at a major intersection.

When the law disobeyed is not the law itself objected to, greater must be the warrant to make the law-breaking morally justifiable. It is one thing to conscientiously refuse to obey a law and accept the punishment; it is something else to use civil disobedience solely as an instrument. The relationship of the conscientious or moral element to the disobedience is much more attenuated in the context of indirect civil disobedience. The social, political, and legal order justifiably react to indirect civil disobedience more severely, reluctant to wink at disobedience merely because a party objects to some other laws or wants to "witness" to something.

There is a hybrid type of civil disobedience neither purely direct nor indirect. An example of this would be the refusal to pay taxes for morally offensive government activity. The parties may not object to the taxing power of government, and may not find any morally objectionable character to the amount of the tax. However, they do object to the way in which government uses that money. The refusal to pay those taxes whether for war or abortion-funding or promotion of secular humanism seems to be somewhere between direct resistance and somewhat artificially connected indirect disobedience.

# FOUR

# Civil Disobedience: As American As Apple Pie

A MERICAN HISTORY IS FRAUGHT with examples of civil disobedience. In essence this country was "born" from civil disobedience. This birthright was recognized by Theodore Parker, a famous abolitionist clergyman, who declared: "Men will call us traitors; what then? That hurt nobody in '76. We are a rebellious nation. Our whole history is treason; our blood was tainted before we were born. . . ." We revel in all our Boston Tea Parties as acts of courageous, principled defiance. The abolition of slavery, the granting of suffrage to women, the blacks' gains in civil rights, and the end of the Vietnam war all owed a debt to vigorous civil disobedience. In all these periods, there were Christians who saw inconsistencies between their faith and government policies and were moved by conscience to act. For them, civil disobedience was holy disobedience. As Daniel Foster, a Massachusetts minister, said in regard to the Fugitive Slave Act, those "who preach that we ought to obey or ought not to disobey this infernal fugitive slave bill, because it has passed both houses of Congress, and received the sanction of the President, . . . in doing so, cast off their allegiance to God." Others were simply people of conscience who were motivated to oppose the government for humanitarian reasons.

## Colonial America

Quakers, those peace-loving folk, did not confuse peace with acquiescence. When their worship was prohibited, they held their meetings anyway and preached their form of the gospel despite the laws to the contrary. They experienced extensive persecution, yet believed that doing so was their duty before God. Their practice of "godly" dissent helped to secure religious liberty in the new nation.

Refusal to pay war taxes in America also has a Quaker heritage. The American Quakers, unlike their British brothers and sisters, made refusal of payment of war taxes a part of their witness to the state. In 1711, William Penn advised the Queen of England that his conscience and his faith would not allow him to pay "a tribute to carry on any war, nor ought any Christian to pay it." In a Quaker pamphlet published in 1715 entitled *Tribute to Caesar* the author argued:

> To pay ordinary taxes is justifiable, of course, and it is not always necessary to inquire what the government does with them. But when taxes are levied specifically for war purposes, and announced as such, the Christian must refuse to pay them. Hence the expedient of voting money "for the queen's use" in response to a demand for military aid is a sacrifice of principle.

In 1755, the Mennonites joined the Quakers in refusing to pay a special tax enacted to support the French and Indian War. They refused to pay the entire tax:

> Though some part of the money to be raised by the said act is said to be for such benevolent purposes, as supporting our friendship with our Indian neighbors, and relieving the distresses of our fellow-subject, ... we could most cheerfully contribute to those purposes, if they were not so mixed, that we cannot in the manner proposed, show our hearty

concurrence therewith, without at the same time assenting to . . . practices, which we apprehend contrary to the testimony which the Lord hath given us to bear.[1]

As a result of their refusal to pay war taxes or assume militia duty these groups were often accused of being disloyal citizens. In response to this criticism, they argued that "Our fidelity to the present government and our willingly paying taxes for purposes which do not interfere with our consciences justly exempt us from the imputation of disloyalty."

## The American Revolution

Tax resistance in colonial America was not limited to the "peace churches." The Boston Tea Party occurred in opposition to a British tax on tea imported into the colonies. Though the people participating were protesting the tax on political rather than religious principles, they helped to establish tax resistance as a historical, perhaps even a "legitimate," means of protest in America.

The Revolutionary War was a severe test of the peace churches' refusal to pay taxes supporting war and their refusal to participate in war. Due to the scarcity of men and money, those who refused to participate in the war were required to pay a tax or send a substitute to fight. Often the land and property of those who refused were seized. If they did not refuse to fight or to pay the tax, many Quakers were expelled from their church's meetings. A schism over this issue occurred in the Mennonite church. Most Mennonites paid fines or went to jail rather than paying their war taxes. Others paid their taxes, designating that they be used for the poor and leaving it to the government's conscience how the money was actually spent. Some simply paid them. Although the members of the peace churches, whether liable for military service or not, were taxed at two or more times the normal rate for being opposed to war and to oath-taking, there is no evidence that they considered resisting these doubled taxes.

The Continental Congress was sympathetic to the problems of the peace churches. On July 18, 1775, it declared that it expected pacifists "to contribute liberally, in this time of universal calamity, to the relief of their disturbed brethren . . . consistently with their religious principles." The Mennonite churches responded that, although they were ready to help those in need or distress, they were unwilling to do or assist in anything by which men's lives were destroyed or hurt.

In contrast to the pacifist notions of the Quakers, Mennonites, and Brethren, there were countless preachers of Puritan, Presbyterian, and other traditions who advocated that the war itself was appropriate civil disobedience. More properly, of course, the Revolutionary War was not so much "civil disobedience" as it was "civil rebellion." But the ease with which Americans legitimized revolution seems to explain our toleration and utilization of the less extreme forms of civil disobedience.

The New England clergy generally taught that as long as the king enforced God's commands, he was owed obedience and assistance. If, however, he violated God's commands, the people had the authority to resist him. While this does not sound much different from what was traditionally taught throughout church history, when these preachers began to talk in terms of the God-given rights of men, their sermons began to have revolutionary implications. The essence of what was said from the pulpit was indistinguishable from what was advocated by secular political theorists. For over 1,300 years, political and ecclesiastical thinking had been closely intertwined. The preachers of the Revolutionary War were merely continuing this tradition.

Many of these preachers viewed violent disobedience as justifiable when citizens' rights were violated. According to Jonathan Mayhew, a Boston minister, for an abused people to "arise unanimously and resist their prince, even to dethrone him is not criminal, but a reasonable way of vindicating their liberties and just rights." David Jones, another early American preacher, discounted a blanket application of the passages in Romans 13 and 1 Peter 2:13-14 and argued that these texts could not be understood to mean obedience to all "despotic ordinances." Rather, "when a people are oppressed, insulted and abused, and can have no other redress, then it becomes our duty as men, with our eyes to God to fight for our liberties and properties. . . ."

The leading Founding Fathers included rationalists or deists who argued for the revolution not from theological perspectives, but from the more scientific principles of republicanism. Their arguments were based primarily on natural law and the rights of men. Yet these arguments, while significant, were probably not what aroused the common man to rebellion. The impetus for rebellion came from other sources, the most important of them being religion. As John Adams said, "The revolution was in the minds and hearts of the people a change in their religious sentiments of their duties and obligations." Religious dedication was at the source of the American Revolution, and it was "fought with the conviction that its outcome was the foreordained will of God." Many Christians believed that the blessings promised to Israel in the Old Testament were prophetic of the future splendor of the United States as a haven for God's people. As a result, "religious energies stimulated, sanctioned and supported the movement for American independence."

While Americans were fighting the British over the issue of submission to taxing power, many were petitioning their own colonial governments for religious liberty and advocating the separation of church and state. One of the primary issues in this battle was over the taxes supporting the established colonial churches and the requirement of filing for a certificate for exemption if one were a minister of another faith. Isaac Backus led the Massachusetts Baptists in their refusal to comply with the laws requiring certification of non-Congregational (non-Puritan) ministers. They opposed the requirement that they apply for exemption, "because the very nature of such a practice implies an acknowledgment that the civil power has a right to set one religious sect up above another." While Backus was not successful in ending the system of certificates of exemption, he no doubt had some influence on the ecclesiastical provisions of the Massachusetts Constitution adopted in 1780.

## The Civil War Period

One cannot discuss the Christian view on civil disobedience in nineteenth-century America without focusing on the abolitionist movement. The abolitionists, most of them Christians or deists, believed that the slavery laws were unjust and could indeed be broken. Pacifists could point to the Sermon on the Mount as the scriptural basis for their position; those who refused to take oaths also had a scriptural basis for their position; the abolitionist Christians seemingly had much of biblical history against them. However, the abolitionists argued that, while scripture does not explicitly prohibit slavery, "God prescribes moral principles incompatible with the practice of slavery." Specifically, they insisted that slavery was incompatible with the command to love our neighbors as ourselves.

While there were many great advocates and practitioners of civil disobedience among the abolitionists, one of the most well-known groups was at Oberlin College in Ohio, which had been greatly influenced by one of its first professors, Charles Finney, a radical evangelist who opposed slavery. The Oberlin community became a leading force in the Underground Railroad and boasted that no slave was ever lost to the federal authorities there. When one slave was captured, students, faculty, and townspeople went to nearby Wellington, and, through sheer numbers, were able to secure his release without violence. After the Wellington Rescue, several were indicted for violation of the Fugitive Slave Act.

Though the group at Oberlin also helped form antislavery parties with candidates in the presidential elections, they advocated that the church should be a militant antislavery tool. Oberlin and many churches split from mainline Presbyterian and Congregational churches over the conservative attitude toward slavery among them. Through Charles Finney, the Oberlin Church imposed religious sanctions to further abolitionism; for example, no slaveholder could partake in the Lord's Supper. The school also trained antislavery ministers, distributed antislavery tracts, and worked to prevent its extension to the territories.

The entire Oberlin community participated in the Underground Railroad. Others were even more militant. Some students even invaded the southern states to help slaves escape to Illinois. They were caught and imprisoned for their activities. Apart from a few incidents, though, one could describe the Oberlin viewpoint as "radical involvement in passive resistance and politics." The individual may owe to a court the most respectful consideration and pondering of its decision; "but when to his mind, after careful, candid examination, God appears to decide against the court, he must act accordingly and submit peacefully to the penalty if he cannot honorably evade it."

Perhaps one of the most committed and prominent New England abolitionists was William Lloyd Garrison. In addition to the abolition of slavery, he advocated opposition to war, abstention from politics, and an end to capital punishment. He did not believe that a Christian should give allegiance to any human government, but that one should not oppose it with force. His views on government bordered on being anarchistic. He was *persona non grata* to many of the abolitionists at Oberlin.

A Unitarian pastor in Boston, John Pierpont, in "A Discourse on the Covenant with Judas," considered the general question of the binding force of agreements to do that which is a violation of natural right. Pierpont compared Judas' covenant with the Pharisees to that of Massachusetts' alleged obligation to Virginia regarding runaway slaves. He declared, "that the morality that compels me to deliver up a fellow man to chains and torture, . . . because others have covenanted for me that I should do so . . . is essentially the morality of a Judas, who would deliver up the Son of Man to be scourged and crucified, because he had covenanted to do so." He argued that we were to consider the rights of man and his Maker's laws above the Constitution. He asked, "Which shall we obey—our dead fathers? or our living God?"

Pierpont's arguments came more clearly into focus with the Fugitive Slave Act in 1850 requiring any United States citizen to participate personally in the capture and return of escaped slaves. The citizens of free states immediately held protest meetings and began to engage in active disobedience of the law. Wendell Phillips called for judges who would "laugh in defiance of the Congress." A Wisconsin state court held the law invalid and ignored attempts to have its decision reviewed by the United States Supreme Court. At one meeting in New York City, a group of free Negroes passed resolutions condemning the act and counseling armed resistance to it. In Canfield, Ohio, a group that included future judges and congressmen passed the following resolution: "Resolved, That, come life or come imprisonment,—come fine or come death—we will neither aid nor assist in the return of any fugitive slave, but, on the contrary, we will harbor and secrete, and by all just means protect and defend him, and thus give him a practical God speed to liberty."[2]

There were others, however, who strongly disagreed with those who advocated disobedience to the Fugitive Slave Act. Civil disobedience became the subject of a broad national debate. Several prominent ministers in the North preached on the duty of citizens to obey their government. At a mass meeting at Faneuil Hall in Boston, a resolution was adopted declaring,

Resolved, That, every species and form of resistance to the execution of a regularly enacted law, except by peaceable appeal to the regular action of the judicial tribunals upon the question of its constitutionality—an appeal which ought never to be opposed or impeded—is mischievous, and subversive of the first principles of social order, and tends to anarchy and bloodshed.[3]

One of the ways in which the abolitionists defied the law was by rescuing fugitive slaves who had been imprisoned. One of the most famous cases was the rescue of Frederick Jenkins, also known as Shadrach. Jenkins, a waiter in a Boston coffee house, was arrested as a fugitive in February 1851. While he was in a federal court room, a group of black men walked in, surrounded him, and hurried him out before his captors realized what happened. One black man and five white abolitionists were eventually arrested and charged with aiding Jenkin's escape. However, they were all exonerated.

The outspoken intentions of many northerners to disregard the law, and the Jenkins rescue, caused President Fillmore to declare that resistance to the Fugitive Slave Law would be considered treason. Warnings of this sort had little effect on the abolitionists. In the Fall of 1851, when a slave holder was killed and his son injured in Pennsylvania while trying to recover four escaped slaves, a federal marshal ordered two Quakers to join a posse to try to recover the slaves and their benefactors. They refused and were arrested along with those suspected of aiding the fugitive slaves. Although their trial received considerable public attention, their acquittal received more.

The organization, if it can be labeled as such, that united many of these people with differing motives and ideologies was the Underground Railroad. The legends have become as much a part of our folklore as of our history. The beginnings of the Railroad may date to the earliest days of our country; George Washington complained about Quakers who helped runaway slaves. Regardless of when it originated, the Railroad continued its humanitarian work right up to and during the Civil War. The number of fugitives transported is estimated as ranging from 75,000 to one million.

Those abolitionists who did harbor and transport often did so at great personal expense. Some had their homes and property damaged by irate southerners and others were subjected to the criminal penalties for assisting the fugitive slaves. In 1837, for example, a federal court in Washington, D.C., convicted a free Negro of forging a certificate of freedom for one slave and a pass for another. He was sentenced to seven years in prison. The Reverend Charles T. Torrey, while in prison for abolitionist activities, developed the idea of a prearranged route for escapees rather than the usual somewhat haphazard improvisations. During the next two years, he helped approximately 400 fugitive slaves to freedom before he was caught and jailed again. Shortly thereafter, he died in prison. Thomas Garrett, a Quaker, is said to have aided more than 2,700 fugitive slaves. He became so well known that his arrest was inevitable. In 1848, when finally apprehended, he accepted without regret a large fine which bankrupted him.

The peace churches faced in their typical manner the question of being obedient to God or man. While they did not appear to have an organized protest against Civil War taxes, perhaps because they viewed the war as an effort to free slaves, they complained that conscientious objection to military service was not really being recognized. In both the North and the South, they faced conscription. Exemption from the draft was possible only by furnishing an acceptable substitute or by paying a bounty of $300 to $500 for hiring one. They argued that it did not seem consistent to hire one man to do what another could not conscientiously do himself. The Quakers were the most vehemently opposed to the fee because "they considered it a tax to obtain religious liberty, which was their inherent right and therefore should not have been offered for a price." Many opted to await the demands of government and pay fines and taxes required of them rather than paying bounty money or attempting to raise it.

## Women's Suffrage and Disobedient Feminists

From 1872, when Susan B. Anthony was arrested for unlawful voting, until the passage of the National Suffrage Amendment in 1919, many otherwise law-abiding women were civil disobedients. In defending their actions, the women used many of the same arguments used by those supporting the Revolutionary War and the abolitionist movement.

Until 1875, when the Supreme Court ruled otherwise, many women felt that no new constitutional amendment was necessary to give women the right to vote. Organizations such as the National Woman Suffrage Association had maintained that women were already enfranchised under the Fourteenth Amendment. Many women had attempted to register to vote, hoping that denials would lead to lawsuits and favorable decisions by the courts. Susan B. Anthony and fourteen other women in Rochester, New York, succeeded in voting in 1872, but they were indicted on criminal charges of "knowingly, wrongfully and unlawfully voting...without a lawful right to vote." As a result, Anthony was convicted and fined $100. Although she told the court that she did not want leniency and that she expected the "full rigors of the law," she refused to pay the fine, alleging as did those in 1776 that it was an unjust claim and that "resistance to tyranny is obedience to God."

In her statement to the court, Anthony compared the situation of women to that of the recently freed slaves: "As then the slaves who got their freedom [had to] take it over, or under, or through the unjust forms of law, precisely so now must women, to get their right to a voice in the government, take it, and I have taken mine and mean to take it at every possible opportunity." She equated the court's denial of her right to vote to "the denial of [her] right of consent as one of the governed, the denial of [her] right to representation as one of the taxed, . . . [and] therefore, the denial of her sacred rights to life, liberty, [and] property."

An amusing yet symbolic story from this period was that of Abby and Julia Smith. These two women did not become active in the suffrage movement until their seventies. Nonetheless, their refusal to pay their property taxes until given a vote at the town meeting gained national attention when they re-purchased their cattle, sold at auctions to satisfy their delin-quent tax bills. They continued this resistance each year for the rest of their lives. At a town meeting, Abby accused the townsmen of being tyrannical and, like Susan B. Anthony, claimed that she and her sister's disobedience was just, since "resistance to tyrants is obedience to God." For "God is a God of justice; men and women stand alike in his sight; he has but one law for both. And why should man [not] have but one law for both, to which both shall be accountable alike?"

In the last years of the suffrage movement, many women were arrested and imprisoned for picketing outside the White House. Although their right to picket was subsequently vindicated by the District of Columbia Court of Appeals, at the time, these women knew that they picketed in the face of certain arrest and likely imprisonment. Initially, the picketing was permitted. However, as their signs became more disturb-ing, they were hassled by onlookers and were finally arrested by police on charges of obstructing traffic even if there were only a few picketers on empty streets. Often the women were fined, and they usually refused to pay because to do so would be an admission of guilt. One of the leaders of the movement even went so far as to say, "We do not wish to make any plea before this court. We do not consider ourselves subject to this court, since as an unenfranchised class, we have nothing to do with the making of the laws which have put us in prison."

On January 10, 1918, one year to the day from the first

appearance of picketers at the White House, the House of Representatives passed the Constitutional Amendment. On June 4, 1919, the National Suffrage Amendment giving women the right to vote was adopted.

## World War I

The most common form of civil disobedience in America during World War I was conscientious objection to military service. There were approximately 20,000 men who initially filed claims to be treated as conscientious objectors in World War I. While most of these were either granted noncombatant status or agreed to serve if their claims were turned down, about 4,000 refused to cooperate, at least initially. However, eventually all but about 500 either entered noncombatant military service, were assigned to war-relief work, or were given furloughs to do farm work. The remaining 500 were court-martialed and convicted. Although none were actually executed, 17 of the 500 were sentenced to death, and 142 were sentenced to life imprisonment. In 1933, President Roosevelt pardoned all those still in prison.

Those who objected to the war and to military service in it had a variety of motives for doing so. Carl Haessler objected for philosophical and political reasons. He pled guilty to violating the compulsory service laws and told the court that the offense was not committed for religious, pacifist, or pro-German reasons. Rather, he felt that "America's participation in the war was unnecessary, of doubtful benefit to the country and to humanity and accomplished largely, though not exclusively, through the pressure of the Allied and American commercial imperialists." He refused noncombatant service on the ground that such service would "give lie to his sincerity." He told the court that he would not complain about the punishment it chose to give him.

Many others objected to the war for religious reasons.

Maurice Hess, a young Quaker who refused to serve, did so on the grounds that the war was contrary to the teachings of Christ. He argued that requiring him to serve in the military was a violation of his religious liberty because it took away his "privilege of living in accordance with the scriptures of God." He told the court that while he desired to make use of his talent out in the world and would be prevented from doing so by being jailed, he knew the importance of obedience to God. For this he was willing to endure as a "true soldier of Christ" whatever punishment was meted out to him.

Like many ministers during the Revolution, a good many preachers in World War I encouraged the patriots to battle in the name of a just cause. However, there were some who did not. John Haynes Holmes, minister of the Community Church of New York, declared in a sermon that, while he would bless those in his congregation who answered the call to arms and pray for them as they performed their duties in the trenches and on the battle fields, he was himself a pacifist. If the draft was adopted, he would decline to serve, regardless of fine, imprisonment, or persecution. He vowed:

> No order of president or governor, no law of nation or state, no loss of reputation, freedom or life, will persuade me or force me to this business of killing. On this issue, for me at least, there is "no compromise." Mistaken, foolish, fanatical, I may be; I will not deny the charge. But false to my own soul I will not be. Therefore here I stand. God help me! I cannot do other![4]

He told his congregation that these views applied to his professional as well as his private life. When the war came he could not preach recruiting sermons, turn the parish house into a drill hall, nor turn church property into a rifle range. Rather, in his church, the Germans would be considered a part of the family of God.

Some, like Roger Baldwin, refused to obey the draft laws on

the grounds that they opposed conscription of life by the state for any purpose, especially for the purpose of conducting war. Baldwin professed, "I cannot consistently, with self-respect, do other than I have, namely, to deliberately violate an act which seems to me to be a denial of everything which ideally and in practice I hold sacred." Although willing to pay the penalty for his view without complaint and refusing to offer a legal defense, he questioned the government's sentencing of some objectors to longer prison terms than many violent criminals.

Perhaps one of the most interesting personalities appearing among the World War I conscientious objectors was Ammon Hennacy. An active member of the Socialist Party, Hennacy advised young men to refuse to register for the draft. Sentenced to two years in prison in Atlanta, he staged a successful boycott over the quality of food served and was put in solitary confinement for the remainder of his term. There, he requested a Bible, since no other reading material was allowed. He read it for a half an hour or so each morning, each afternoon, and each evening until he had read it through four times.

Hennacy wanted to be a force for change in the world. He decided that violence, assassination, and revolution were not the way. He recalled that Daniel, Peter, and Paul were each victorious in their own fashions through peaceful means. Jesus who "was confronted with a whole world empire of tyranny and chose not to overturn the tyrant and make Himself King, but to change the hatred in the hearts of men to love and understanding to overcome evil with goodwill." Finally, the Sermon on the Mount became compelling to him, and he saw that the world operated on principles opposite to those expressed by Jesus.

After eight-and-a-half months in solitary, Hennacy was released on parole. Immediately arrested again for refusing to register for a draft held while he was jailed, he was taken to a county jail to await trial. At his trial, he was asked whether he would again refuse to register in the next draft. He replied that he had entered prison as an atheist who would not fight in a capitalist war and that he had since read Tolstoy's *The Kingdom of God Is Within You,* and had become an anarchist. When the judge asked him what an anarchist was, he replied that "An anarchist is one who doesn't have to have a cop to make him behave." He told the judge that one simply had to obey God rather than man. The judge dismissed the case immediately. Both Hennacy and his lawyer were shocked. "I approached the court this time with love for my enemy and had never thought I would get my freedom."

## Civil Disobedience and the Organization of Labor

The attempt of labor to organize in the early part of the twentieth century met with frustration not only from employers, but from law enforcement officials. Many were jailed for their participation in strikes and sit-downs as well as for speaking out on the worker's plight. Violence erupted in the unionizing effort on both sides. Employers resisting unionization would hire thugs to "inhibit" those suspected of unionizing. Once unions were established and strikes held, strike breakers or scabs were often the objects of violence by the union members.

The Industrial Workers of the World (IWW) was one of the organizations that had to contend with law enforcement officials. For example, in Spokane, Washington, members of the IWW insisted on speaking on the streets in front of an employment agency's offices about the agency's deceptive practices. About 500 to 600 men were thrown in prison for their speeches. Several were killed and others died from pneumonia while in prison. Those remaining in jail were eventually released on the condition that the IWW did not prosecute the officers for their maltreatment of the prisoners.

In 1915, in Sioux City, Iowa, the police arrested several IWW members without warrant. The next day, they were each sentenced either to a fine of $100 or to sixty days in jail. They opted for jail and the story spread through the country. Members of the union headed for Sioux City. As they entered town, they were arrested. The Sioux City jails were soon crowded to capacity. While in jail, they refused to work and went on a hunger strike. The city officials capitulated. The prisoners were released and the officials in Sioux City guaranteed free-speech rights to union members to discuss their views.

The attempts by the Congress of Industrial Organizations (CIO) also encountered considerable resistance challenging the legality of their activities. One of their activities that met with opposition was the sit-down strike. In a sit-down, the workers refused to work or to leave their factories, literally living in the factories. These strikes were particularly popular in the 1930s. Like the civil rights demonstrators in the 1960s, the strikers were accused of trespassing on private property.

One of the most famous sit-down strikes began in December 1937 in Flint, Michigan. The United Auto Workers Union had made several attempts to obtain recognition and a union contract from General Motors. Frustrated by the lack of progress, a strike was ordered at the Fisher Body Plant. In less than two months, the weekly production of cars was about 2.5 percent of normal and almost all General Motors employees were idle. About one month after the strike began, a federal district court issued an injunction restraining the workers from continuing to remain in the plant, from picketing, and from interfering in any manner with those who wanted to work. The strikers refused to obey the sheriff's orders to leave.

In mid-January with the workers still in possession of the plant, the company adopted more violent tactics. With the help of the company and city police, GM tried to starve and freeze the workers out of the plant, by setting up barricades to prevent any food from being delivered to the strikers and by turning off the heat. Tear-gas bombs were thrown at the strikers by the police, who also used clubs and riot guns in their effort to gain control of the plant. Although several strikers were injured and had to be hospitalized, the workers retained control of the plant. The wounded were arrested on their release from the hospital. Seven of the strike leaders were among those arrested, charged with unlawful assembly and malicious destruction of property.

Shortly after this incident, the company finally agreed to recognize the UAW and scheduled a conference to negotiate a contract on the condition that the workers evacuate the plant. Just before the strikers evacuated the Fisher plant, the conference was cancelled. The union then decided to stage another sit-down at a Chevrolet plant also in Flint. A second injunction was issued, this time ordering the union officers and the strikers to evacuate the plant within twenty-four hours or be penalized fifteen million dollars. The strikers refused and the judge ordered them all arrested. The local sheriff, lacking a sufficient number of deputies, was unable to do so. On February 11, an agreement was reached and the strike ended. The workers, who had disobeyed court orders, were victorious in their struggle for safe working conditions and fair wages. After living in the Fisher plant for forty-four days, they marched out carrying an American flag and singing "Solidarity Forever."

Despite the success of this form of strike, it was still illegal in the courts under the law of trespass. At the time, the supporters of the sit-down argued that this should not unduly concern labor, since most weapons used by it were initially found to be illegal. The issue, as articulated by Rabbi Edward L. Israel, former Chairman of the Social Justice Commission of the Central Conference of American Rabbis, was one of human rights versus property rights. He declared that:

> The ethical issue in the sit-down strike concerns itself with the right of an employee to his job. According to the average standard of wages in industry today, practically every

working family is only a few days removed from starvation. We must therefore ask ourselves whether the right of hiring and firing, at a time when jobs are at a premium, can possibly be construed to be surrounded by such absolutistic and unassailable property prerogatives that it can literally place within the hands of an employer the power of life and death over the men who work for him.[5]

Homer Martins, president of the Automobile Workers Union, has argued that the worker has property rights to his job: "This property right involves the right to support his family, feed his children and keep starvation away from the door. This property right is the very foundation stone of American homes."

## World War II, Conscientious Objectors

Although war-tax resistance was minimal during World War I, it became a larger issue in the Second World War. The amount of money spent for the war was unprecedented. The consciousness of many who opposed war was pricked by a 10 percent defense tax added onto their 1941 income tax returns. Many refused to pay this extra tax. The federal government also required that every automobile display a defense tax stamp which cost $7.09. In 1942, Edward Bromley and several other pacifists refused to pay for the stamp. He was jailed for sixty days. To protest his conviction, several cars without stamps were parked outside of the courthouse on the day of his sentencing. After two years, the law was rescinded. However, in general, there was not much interest in nonpayment during World War II and there was no organized war tax resistance movement.

Fewer conscientious objectors seem to have been jailed during World War II than during the previous war. The Burke-Wadsworth legislation had provided that conscientious objectors could satisfy their obligations by working at civilian public service camps. Nonetheless, there were those who for religious or ethical reasons would not comply with the registration law. In a joint statement Donald Benedict, David Dellinger, and six other students at Union Theological Seminary explained that "It is our positive proclamation as followers of Jesus Christ that we must overcome evil with good. We seek in our daily living to reconcile that separation of man from man and man from God which produces war." They refused to obey the conscription law because it was a part of the institution of war. Exemptions did not compensate for the fact that as conscientious objectors they were complying with an act whose purpose was the militarization of America. They were sentenced to a year and a day in jail.

Another Christian pacifist, Leon Thompson, believed that at the heart of the conscription issue was a question of loyalty. "The cleavage between my loyalty to God and to the State is at stake. I grant the right of the State to conscript property, under due process of law. . . . The State may even forcibly restrain my physical body. But the United States government did not create me; God did that. I must account to God for the real me, since man is a spiritual being. . . ."

Many conscientious objectors agreed to comply with the Burke Wadsworth Bill's registration requirements and take part in noncombatant service because of Adolf Hitler and the atrocities he committed. Albert Einstein was initially an ardent pacifist opposed to war in any form. In his famous "Two Percent" speech given in 1930, he predicted that resistance by 2 per cent of the eligible manpower of the nation would make war impossible. Conscription laws would be unenforcable. By 1933, the persecution and militarism in Nazi Germany caused Einstein to change his mind. Although many pacifists were outraged by his change in posture, others were convinced by his argument that to remain pacifist in the face of Hitler's tactics was to "give up the defense of culture." Einstein warned that:

To prevent the greater evil, it is necessary that the lesser evil—the hated military—be accepted for the time being. Should German armed might prevail, life will not be worth living anywhere in Europe.... In the present circumstance, realistic pacifists should no longer advocate the destruction of military power; rather, they should strive for its internationalization.[6]

As a result of these views, he was declared an enemy of the state by the Nazis. He took up residence in Princeton, New Jersey, and, in 1940, became an American citizen.

## The Civil Rights Movement

Although subsequent chapters discuss the civil rights movement at great length in terms of Martin Luther King's nonviolent approach, a few comments here may help to put the period in context. While Martin Luther King was certainly one of the most important, if not the most important leader of the civil rights movement, he was not alone. Many other organizations and their leadership did not adopt King's nonviolent approach to redressing the wrongs of segregation and prejudice. Some viewed nonviolence as too slow, while others considered it inappropriate to their ends of establishing a black nationalist state.

One of these outspoken leaders was Stokely Carmichael, who became the national chairman of the Student Nonviolent Coordinating Committee (SNCC) in 1966. Carmichael and other black leaders remind us that violence can be and is often part and parcel of civil disobedience. Though King had been instrumental in founding the organization in 1960, SNCC did not remain true to the principle of nonviolence, its name, or its statement of purpose which declared: "We affirm the philosophical or religious ideal of nonviolence as the foundation of our purpose, the presupposition of our faith and the manner of our action. Nonviolence as it grows from the

Judaeo-Christian tradition seeks a social order permeated by love."

Under Stokely Carmichael's leadership, the organization moved away from nonviolence to more belligerent and radical means, from disobedience to a revolutionary posture. Carmichael talked of "black power" and of the inherent corruption of the political institutions of this country. At Berkeley in 1968, he announced his intentions to fight "fire with fire" and if the police played Gestapo with submachine guns, the blacks would play back with them. He complained that he was tired of trying to prove things to white people and waiting to get the civil rights that they deserved. If things did not happen soon, he said, "we have no choice but to say very clearly, move on over, or we're goin to move you over."

Black leaders such as Malcolm X and Elijah Muhammad argued that there could be no civil rights, no racial equality, and no successful desegregation in this country. They had grown impatient with the nonviolent means of King and his followers. Instead, they advocated the formation of a black nationalist state. They told their followers that not only was the white man their enemy but also that they should riot, burn, and kill to accomplish their goals. The actions they encouraged were really uncivil "disobedience."

Despite the activities of the more violent groups in the civil rights movement, there were those, like Bayard Ruskin, who maintained their commitment to nonviolence. After viewing the violence and destruction in the Harlem riots, Ruskin became an outspoken proponent of nonviolence. Often, however, these leaders did not have the same notions of nonviolence as did King. Many viewed it not as a way of life, but as a practical political tool. In a speech to the Fellowship of Reconciliation in 1964, Ruskin questioned King's theory that love in return for hate was a viable option. Ruskin advocated a strategic nonviolence that would not turn its back on the Negro who resorted to violence:

The Negro who resorts to violence will get our moral support, financial support and support in the courts, because it is wrong to turn one's back on people who have been so demoralized and trampled on that they literally have no choice except to fight back, and then turn to them and say that was naughty. We have got to make that clear or we have no ability to sell what we truly mean when we say love.[7]

## *Vietnam War Protest Movement*

The social and political upheaval of the 60s was not confined to race relations. Just when it seemed that the country was finally cooling off from the summer of '64, the war protest movement erupted in proportions heretofore unparalleled in peace movements in this country. Never had a military effort aroused so much opposition from such varied sectors of society. While World Wars I and II could be legitimized by claims like "we are making the world safe for democracy," or "the atrocities of Nazism required that the nation get involved," the Vietnam War was not so clearly supportable.

Initially, the religious antiwar sentiment came from predictable sources, the peace churches and pacifists. One of the first organized actions taken was in 1965 when 6,000 people signed a "Declaration of Conscience Against the War in Vietnam." This declaration was adopted at a time when most Americans were still supporting this country's presence in Southeast Asia. The signers of the document declared their refusal to cooperate with the government in the war, and to serve in the armed forces or take part in the manufacture or development of military equipment. They vowed to encourage acts of civil disobedience to stop the flow of soldiers and munitions to Southeast Asia. The following note was placed at the bottom of the Declaration to serve as a warning to those who signed or distributed it.

Signing or distributing this Declaration of Conscience might be construed as a violation of the Universal Military Training and Service Act, which prohibits advising persons facing the draft to refuse service. Penalties of up to five years imprisonment, and/or of $5,000 are provided. While prosecutions under this provision of the law almost never occur, persons signing or distributing this declaration should face the possibility of serious consequences.[8]

The Declaration of Conscience was the beginning of an unarmed battle to end the Vietnam War. Although declarations are often largely symbolic, it was not long before this one was translated into action. The summer and fall of 1967 saw the burgeoning of opposition to America's involvement in Vietnam. The Resistance, a national movement opposing the war by advocating draft resistance, declared October 16, 1967, the day when all those opposed to the draft would either burn their draft cards or return them to the Selective Service. As a part of the protest, the Arlington Street Church in Boston held a Service of Conscience and Acceptance. At that service, some fifty men burned their draft cards and several times that number gave their cards to clergy who sent them to the government. Several participants in this "service" were indicted on charges of criminal conspiracy. One of the speakers, Michael Faber, a graduate student in English at Harvard, was arrested for his sermon, "A Time to Say No." He told his audience that each of their acts of returning or burning their draft cards was their personal no to the government, not necessary for their personal moral integrity but for the message it conveyed. It was vital to be the moral person whose thinking leads to political action rather than the moral person who is only led to personal sinlessness. Faber was realistic. He said, "We must not confuse the ceremony and symbolism of today's service with the reality that we are only a few hundred people with very little power." Yet, he argued, they must act to uphold "the great tradition within the church and synagogue which has always struggled against . . . the worldly forces that have always been in control."

Faber was found guilty, fined $1,000 and sentenced to two years in jail. He appealed the decision in 1969 and his conviction was overturned.

The most notorious act of civil disobedience during this era was that of the Catonsville Nine, a group which included Daniel and Phillip Berrigan. On May 17, 1968, seven Catholic men and two Catholic women destroyed the files of those eligible for registration at a Selective Service office in Catonsville, Maryland, by pouring home-made napalm on them and setting fire to them. Then they waited for the police. At their trial, they contended that they were innocent because their act was, in the long run, a beneficial one. It was an attempt to obstruct an "immoral" war and to protect America from this destructive process. Their "innocence" was rejected by the court. They were convicted for having destroyed government property and were sentenced to terms of two to four years.

The Catonsville Nine were concerned with transforming society. They viewed their act as "an act beyond politics; a religious act, a liturgical act; an act of witness." They believed that "If only a small number of men could offer this kind of witness it would purify the world." The Berrigans wrote extensively on civil disobedience. On of their best-known pieces is Daniel's play "The Trial of the Catonsville Nine." In the play, he is quite critical of the Christian community's response to the Vietnam War. He wrote, "They embrace their society with all their heart and abandon the cross. They pay lip service to Christ and military service to the powers of death."

In the play, Daniel responds to the judge's question regarding his brother's act of pouring blood on the draft file.

from the beginning of our republic
good men had said no

acted outside the law
when conditions so demanded
And if a man did this
time might vindicate him show his act to be lawful
a gift to society
a gift to history
and to the community
A few men must have a long view
must leave history to itself
to interpret their lives their repute[9]

Does all of this—sit-ins, abolitionism, war protests—make civil disobedience as American as apple pie? Well, maybe not. But civil disobedience has been claimed as a moral right, albeit not a constitutional one, since the beginning of this country. It has always been a reaction against persecution of some form or another by those who have felt that there was a higher law to which they owed allegiance. Most often it gained prominence where the moral issues were indeed powerful, perhaps compelling. As one would expect in a nation committed to governance by the people these actions have often been effective. The continued willingness of the Quakers to endure persecution in New England resulted in religious liberty. The abolitionists protested long and loud until finally a war was fought to end slavery in this country. The labor unionists, women's suffragettes, and blacks disobeyed to end economic exploitation, ballot box discrimination, and racial segregation. Those who remained firm in their refusal to support war have won more liberal laws regarding conscientious objectors. History is often merciless to those who were slow to grant these rights. Yet, there is some comfort in knowing that it requires monumental commitment and dedication on the part of those involved to force these changes. Our society, while malleable, cannot be changed on a whim.

Those who would easily dismiss civil disobedience as the

acts of malcontents must weigh whether or not the fabric of life today is not more just and more moral because some had the will to say no, because they respected the concept of law so highly they refused to let it rest in injustice.

# FIVE

# Thoreau, Gandhi, and King: The Legacy of Creative Protest

## *Henry David Thoreau*

In many ways, Henry David Thoreau seems ill-matched with the rich and powerful historical figures of Mahatma Gandhi and Martin Luther King. More a recluse than an active social reformer, Thoreau seemed simply to want to escape from mankind and find his personal peace at Walden Pond. His own civil disobedience pales in comparison to the dynamism and the energy released by the acts of Gandhi or King. One night in jail for refusing to pay a local poll tax would hardly seem sufficient to join the ranks of the courageous. Yet, Thoreau's essay "Civil Disobedience," written in response to his arrest, became not only his most influential work, but a philosophical posture which deeply influenced Gandhi and King, and thus has forever placed his name in the gallery of the civil-disobedience heroes.

While Thoreau was a religious man, he was not clearly a Christian. He was a part of the New England Transcendental-ist Movement, a group which reacted against the orthodoxy of Calvinism. Transcendentalists believed in God but tended to reject the deity of Christ. They focused on the immanence of the divine, individualism, mysticism, reformism, and optimism regarding human nature.[1] Like the abolitionists at Oberlin, they preached that there was a higher law than manmade law to which man was subject. Thoreau and Ralph Waldo Emerson, another famous transcendentalist author, insisted upon "the prerogatives of the individual in defiance of the will of the rulers of the state."[2] Thoreau argued that civil law, particularly that concerning moral issues, was an unwarranted encroachment by the government into the rights of the individual.

It was this view that led him to refuse to pay the poll tax in protest of the federal government's position on slavery and its involvement in the Mexican War, which he viewed as a slaveholders' plot to enlarge their influence. According to Thoreau, those who opposed these should do more than speak; they should refuse to sustain the unjust government which protected the slaveholders and made the war. To act otherwise was to sacrifice one's integrity. Therefore, when the sheriff demanded the tax, which had not been paid for six years, and promised jail if it was not paid, Thoreau responded that there was "no time like the present." After one night in jail, a friend paid the tax, contrary to his desires.

In the opening paragraph of "Civil Disobedience" Thoreau adopts as his own the motto "That which governs best is that which governs least." In fact, he insisted "That government is best is that which governs not at all." He thought that a man's conscience should enable him to determine what was right and that there would be no need for civil government except to control practical affairs such as road building. However, he realized that in reality man was not and probably never would be ready for this sort of "nongovernment."

Thoreau believed that the ideal government was one where there was true respect for the individual. While he felt that the evolution of government from absolute monarchy to democracy was progress in this direction, he did not feel that democracy was necessarily the last possible improvement. He questioned the infallibility of majority rule, since the majority could make unjust laws. Most men, he insisted, held law too sacred. One should cultivate not so much respect for the law as respect for the right. "Law never made men a whit more just and, by means of their respect for it, even the most well-disposed are daily made the agents of injustice."

Unlike those who relied on his essay in the years to come, Thoreau did not have a social reform agenda or the desire to organize others to follow him. To be free of mankind was his goal. Living at Walden Pond symbolized this goal. It was his escape, and by doing odd jobs here and there when he needed money, he was not so dependent on society and its government as are most men. He merely asked that the state let him alone. When it did not and by means of laws such as the Fugitive Slave Act asked him to become a slave catcher, then the state did become his concern. It had violated his moral integrity. To withdraw and stand aloof from the government was the only solution for a man with moral integrity.

He did not care to trace the course of his tax dollar to determine whether it bought a musket. He was concerned, rather, to trace the effects of his allegiance. While he realized that he could not oppose the force of the State singlehandedly, he hoped that his passive resistance might change the minds of men who exercised power. His commitments if adopted by many, would achieve social change. He said,

> [A] minority is powerless while it conforms to the majority; it is not even a minority then; but it is irresistible when it clogs by its whole weight. If the alternative is to keep all men in prison, or give up war and slavery, the state will not hesitate which to choose. If a thousand men were not to pay their tax-bills this year, that would not be a violent and bloody measure as it would be to pay them, and enable the state to commit violence and shed innocent blood.[3]

While Thoreau's personal choice concerning the proper form of disobedience was passive, there is some reason to think that he also condoned and even practiced more active forms of resistance. In "Civil Disobedience," he declares that "when a sixth of the population of a nation that has undertaken to be the refuge of liberty are slaves, and a whole country is unjustly overrun and conquered by a foreign army and subjected to military law, I think that it is not too soon for honest men to rebel and revolutionize."

There is also evidence that he actively participated in the Underground Railroad. A fugitive slave from Virginia, Henry Williams, fled Boston as the police closed in on him. He showed up at the Thoreau residence with a letter from William Lloyd Garrison. The Thoreau family hid him until funds could be raised for train fare to Canada. In 1853, Thoreau assisted another fugitive slave and spent a day bathing his sores prior to sending him across the border. In breaking the laws under the Fugitive Slave Act, Thoreau's disobedience was an active one.

By 1851, it seems clear that Thoreau would even sanction violence to end slavery. With regard to Captain John Brown, the violent and bloody Puritan abolitionist who led the raid on Harper's Ferry, Thoreau commented that "(i)t was [Brown's] peculiar doctrine that a man has a perfect right to interfere by force with a slaveholder, in order to rescue the slave. I agree with him." In response to John Brown's arrest, trial, and certain execution, Thoreau wrote another of his famous essays entitled "A Plea for Captain John Brown." It is not clear that Thoreau was really making a serious argument for saving John Brown as much as he was talking about the necessity for civil disobedience to end the evil of slavery. While Brown was on trial, Thoreau wrote in his journal, "I do not wish to kill or be killed, but I can forsee circumstances in which both of these things would be by me unavoidable." Thus, it seems that Thoreau's nonviolent resistance was due more to his personality than to a philosophical commitment to nonviolence.

When was such resistance justified? Thoreau did not advocate disunion with the state over every injustice which might occur. In "Civil Disobedience" he provided something of a formula which would help one determine when resistance to injustice is justified:

> If the injustice is part of the necessary friction of the machine of government, let it go, let it go; perchance it will wear smooth—certainly the machine will wear out. If the injustice has a spring or a pulley, or a rope or a crank, exclusively for itself then perhaps you may consider whether the remedy will not be worse than the evil; but if it is of such a nature that it requires you to be the agent of injustice to another, then I say break the law. Let your life be a counterfriction to stop the machine. What I have to do is to see at any rate, that I do not lend myself to the wrong that I condemn.[4]

Thus, according to Thoreau, one should break the law only if it requires one to act unjustly toward another.

Thoreau's thoughts on civil disobedience influenced the thoughts of many others who chose to resist their governments. Perhaps the most famous of these was the Indian lawyer turned civil resister, Mahatma Gandhi. "Civil Disobedience" has often been referred to as Gandhi's source book in his South African campaign. In Gandhi's appeal to "American Friends" he wrote, "You have given me a teacher in Thoreau who furnished me through his essay on the 'Duty of Civil Disobedience,' scientific conformation of what I was doing in South Africa." Gandhi also stated to Roger Baldwin that the essay contained the essence of his political philosophy, not only as India's struggle related to the British, but as to his own view of the relation of citizens to government.

Thoreau's essay was also to influence the thoughts of civil rights leader, Martin Luther King, Jr.:

During my early college days I read Thoreau's essay for the first time. Fascinated by the idea of refusing to cooperate with an evil system, I was so deeply moved that I read the work several times. I became convinced then that non-cooperation with evil is as much a moral obligation as is cooperation with good. No other person has been more eloquent and passionate in getting this idea across than Henry David Thoreau. As a result of his writings and personal witness we are the heirs of a legacy of creative protest. It goes without saying that the teachings of Thoreau are more alive today than ever before. Whether expressed in a sit-in, at lunch counters, a freedom ride in Mississippi, a peaceful protest in Albany, Georgia, or a bus boycott in Montgomery, Alabama, it is an outgrowth of Thoreau's insistence that evil must be resisted and no moral man can patiently adjust to injustice.[5]

Other Americans have looked to Thoreau as the symbol of resistance to oppressive laws. In Groton, Connecticut, a rowboat used in demonstrations against nuclear submarines was christened the *Henry David Thoreau*. Those who have refused to pay their taxes in opposition to war have sent copies of "Civil Disobedience" to the Internal Revenue Service. Marchers protesting at a missile base in Kansas pointed to Thoreau as justification for their conduct.

Thoreau was not and is not without his critics however. Henry Canby, in his biography of Thoreau, says that, "If the individual is to determine his own rights, what authority is left to distinguish between enlightened resistance to rulers of a state and anarchy which will eventually dissolve the state itself."[6] To his friend Emerson, Thoreau's experience in jail was "mean and sulking, and in bad taste." One writer observed that, for some, "Civil Disobedience serves as the classic document for signing a separate peace treaty and resigning from society." Perhaps one of the best statements regarding the problem of the extreme individualism advocated by

Thoreau comes from Henry Eulau of Stanford: "Thoreau's philosophy should warn us of the dilemma into which he fell and from which he could not escape because he returned time and time again to individual conscience as the ultimate reality . . . and he did not realize how . . . dangerous the moral can be."

Thus, while Thoreau has been heralded as the great and classic disobedient of his time, it is clear that his actions were based solely on his personal conscience. This form of un-bridled disobedience is not entirely adoptable by Christians today. Many Christians would agree with Thoreau that we are all subject to a law higher than man's and that it is a just person's duty to disobey an unjust law and to bear the consequences of that disobedience. In this way, the individual can remain true to his conscience and be a "witness" to the state. However, Thoreau's notion that all civil law which concerned moral issues was an encroachment on the rights of the individual is more controversial. It would seem to require disobedience of many laws that we regard as just and fair. Adoption of such a philosophy would also require the abandonment of the public and political agenda of both the Christian right and left and would seem to reject the notion that the government has certain moral duties.

Moreover, Thoreau's insistence on the individual con-science in determining whether to obey or disobey a given law or to engage in an illegal form of protest (nonpayment of taxes) minimizes the role of the Christian community and church. His individualism ignores the importance of the counsel of and consensus within the body of believers which may give authority to disobey the law. Finally, Thoreau's individualistic form of civil disobedience fails to initiate social change towards justice. Thoreau showed no inclination to work through the political system to achieve justice while protesting. Nonetheless, "he sang out in nonviolent defiance, but how few men since could carry the tune."[7]

## Mahatma Gandhi

Richard Attenborough's award winning film, *Gandhi,* has catapulted the life of this slight Indian leader, who led his country to independence from Great Britain without an army, into even greater worldwide acclaim. Although he was already famous, the film dramatized the plight of the Indian people and Gandhi's amazing ability to inspire men, women, and children to battle nonviolently. Nonetheless, Richard Grenier called the film a "pious fraud" for its historical inaccuracies and deification of Gandhi.[8] Not everyone in India was pleased with the film, and riots broke out over its showing. Despite these criticisms the film correctly portrays Gandhi as a powerful spiritual and political leader with a revolutionary means of attaining his ends. More than any other figure, Gandhi's writings and acts have established the character and credibility of civil disobedience. He was the first to engage in nonviolent action on a large scale to achieve a political end. Due to his efforts, nonviolent action was soon perceived as a technique capable of taking the initiative in an active struggle. In essence, Gandhi forged a link between a means of mass struggle and a moral preference for nonviolence.

**The Basics of Gandhian Resistance.** Unlike Thoreau, Gandhi's form of disobedience could not be referred to as "unbridled." He developed an entire philosophy of nonviolent resistance known as *Satyagraha,* meaning the "firmness" which comes from truth. It is a philosophy which not only governs one's approach to civil disobedience but to one's life as well. Gandhian nonviolence is to enter into the very fiber of one's being and revolutionize all sides of one's life. In a sense, Gandhi subscribed to nonviolence as a religion. To him Truth is God and the way to discover him is to practice nonviolence in all aspects of one's life. Thus, Satyagraha is a creed, not a mere policy—an end, not simply a tactic. According to Gandhi, it did not avail to those who adopted it simply as a last resort and who did not possess a living faith in the God of Love. However, Grenier correctly notes the danger in assuming that Gandhi's God was the Western, Christian God. Rather, Gandhi's notion of God probably combined what he believed to be the best of Eastern and Western traditions.

Essential to Gandhian thought is the *character* of persons who act, not merely their *method*. Satyagraha was not simply an instrument to be used when force was impossible, but as a weapon superior to force. Gandhi felt that certain prerequisites must be satisfied before anyone could engage in it. Perhaps the requirements for a Satyagrahi (one who practices Satyagraha) are best described by its inventor.

Satyagraha presupposes self-discipline, self-control, self-purification, . . . A Satyagrahi must never forget the distinction between evil and the the evil-doer. He must not harbour ill-will or bitterness against the latter. He may not even employ needlessly offensive language against the evil person, however unrelieved his evil might be. For it should be an article of faith with every Satyagrahi that there is none so fallen in this world but can be converted by love. A Satyagrahi will always try to overcome evil by good, anger by love, untruth by truth, hisma (violence) by ahisma (nonviolence). There is no other way of purging the world of evil. Therefore the person who claims to be a Satyagrahi always tries by close and prayerful self-introspection and self-analysis to find out whether he is himself completely free from the taint of anger, ill-will and such other human infirmities, whether he is not himself capable of those very evils against which he is out to lead a crusade. In self-purification and penance lies half the victory of a Satyagrahi. A Satyagrahi has faith that the silent and undemonstrative action of truth and love that produces far more permanent and abiding results than speeches or such other showy performances.[9]

It is obvious that the first prerequisite for the Satyagrahi is to embrace nonviolence as a permanent approach to life. The Satyagrahi must also be willing to tolerate many laws even when doing so is inconvenient. Thus, he acquires the right to disobey the manifestly unjust laws. Lastly, the Satyagrahi must be willing to suffer for his position. He must be willing to act and to persist in the face of severe repression or danger to his property, family, or person.

Once the people are prepared, the nonviolent campaign can be implemented. The first stage is recognition of the radical wrongness of a situation. The Satyagrahi must reach a precise understanding of what is wrong and the evil underlying that wrong so that a stand can be made there. After the wrong is discovered, the next stage is to refuse to submit to the wrong or to cooperate with it. Gandhi urged, however, that before any action took place the people must attempt to bring the wrong home to the law-giver by petition and the like. If such efforts fail, then the Satyagrahi could fast; engage in strikes, boycotts, and mass marches; or disobey a given law. In this manner a moral pressure is exerted on the state to rectify its evils.

It is apparent that Gandhi's Satyagraha is not just another name for civil disobedience. While civil disobedience may be a part or branch of Satyagraha, all Satyagraha (such as fasting or legal strikes) is not civil disobedience. Unlike civil disobedience, whose end may be the removal of an unjust law or practice, the end of Satyagraha is the opponent's conversion. It thus presumes a certain openness to moral conviction on the part of the law makers. The appeal is to conscience, justice, and morality. The method is intended to awaken the higher sensitivities of both the oppressed and the oppressor. In its purest form, Satyagraha is not so much coercive as it is educational and persuasive.

**South Africa and the Beginnings of Satyagraha.** Gandhi did not arrive at his formula for nonviolent action overnight. He grew up in a prominent Indian family of a respectable caste. After completing his schooling in India, he studied law in London. It was in London that he was exposed to Western thought and gained a respect for the British. After completing his studies, he returned to India to practice law. Unable to speak articulately in the courtroom, it soon became clear that he was not going to succeed. Leaving his wife and children in India, he went to South Africa to act as legal counsel for a prominent Indian businessman. It was through his encounter with racism in South Africa that he began to develop his thoughts on nonviolent action.

During this time Gandhi was also on a spiritual quest. He read the Bible and a great deal of Christian literature, and was moved by Christ's precept to "resist not evil." While Gandhi never became a Christian, he did recognize as truth much of what Christ said. He was particularly influenced by Tolstoy's view that the state and the class hierarchy are evil and, therefore, that the Christian rebel must withdraw from injustice, be nonviolent, and try to convert the ruling class. To Gandhi, Tolstoy was expounding the Hindu concept of nonviolence, *ahisma*, with greater precision than did the Hindus. Ahisma to Hindus was little more than not injuring other creatures: it was essentially passive. Tolstoy's expression of the concept in New Testament terms showed Gandhi how rules of action might be deduced from it. He began to see nonviolence as a means of effecting change.

The beauty of Satyagraha was that all of society, even women and children could be effective participants. It was the government itself which gave him this insight when a South African Supreme Court held that Hindu, Muslim, and Parsee marriages were invalid, treating Indian wives as concubines and making them subject to deportation. When the government told thousands of women that they were living in sin and that their children were bastards, they began demonstrating in the hope of being arrested.

Gandhi always warned his adversaries before he acted. When

no response was forthcoming, the Indians acted as promised; women were rounded up by the police and sentenced to hard labor.

During this campaign Gandhi once cancelled a mass march because of a strike by white railway workers, declaring as a principle that the Satyagrahis would not take advantage of an opponent's accidental difficulties. The impact on public opinion was overwhelming, and, in 1914, the government leaders capitulated and reinstated the status of Indian women.

Gandhian nonviolence seemingly triumphed, but in terms of the goals of Satyagraha the success was only partial. Gandhi had won political concessions but he had not changed the hearts of his adversaries. The protest never really ousted white racist supremacy in South Africa. The settlement alleviated many discriminatory laws. However, other laws still stood. After Gandhi left South Africa for India in 1915, many of the gains were lost.

Gandhi's success in South Africa established Satyagraha as an effective tool whereby rights could be secured by personal suffering. It also established him as a spiritual hero and an important political figure in India. To the masses he became the *Mahatma* or "Great Soul," someone who embodies the indwelling spirit of all life in an especially high and noble form. As a Mahatma he had the ability to sway the masses as no one else could, and therefore he became the most indispensible politician of all.

**India: Satyagraha for Freedom.** The India to which Gandhi returned in 1915 was very different from the India he had left years before. The Indian National Congress had demanded home rule from the British in 1906. A nationalist spirit was growing throughout the country and was beginning to filter down to the masses by the time he returned. In this political and social climate, Gandhi's Satyagraha faced a greater challenge than in South Africa where it was used by a minority against a few specific laws. Could Satyagraha actually alleviate the oppression of a whole nation and achieve home rule? Initially, most of India's nationalist leadership were skeptical.

**Experiments at the Local Level.** To illustrate Satyagraha as a way of life, Gandhi established an *ashram* or lay community, whose residents were committed to nonviolence as a way of life. They took vows embodying principles which Gandhi felt every Satyagrahi should follow in his daily life: truth, non-violence, chastity, non-possessiveness, fearlessness, control of the palate, equality of religion, anti-untouchability, and the use of goods made in India. Gandhi viewed revival of the cottage industries in India such as handspinning and hand-weaving as a form of Satyagraha. He perceived them as a nonviolent challenge to economic oppression. To Gandhi, taking the vows was a necessary sign of the strength required for one to become an effective Satyagrahi. He felt that one should "never doubt the necessity of vows for the purpose of self-purification and self-realization."

With the ashram in place, Gandhi used Satyagraha to help the poor and oppressed. In 1918, Gandhi encouraged a group of farmers to refuse to pay a tax on their crops because they were impoverished from a crop failure. In general, Gandhi urged caution when undertaking such a venture, because "We must not be indifferent about violence and we must make sure of the masses exercising self-control whilst they are witness to the confiscation of their crops and cattle and to the forfeiture of their holdings."[10]

**Satyagraha as a National Effort.** After several successful experiences with Satyagraha on specific, local issues, Gandhi was faced with a new and greater challenge on the national level. The Rowlatt legislation provided that cases of sedition could be tried without a jury. Sedition could include having a nationalist leaflet in one's pocket. Gandhi viewed this as a severe restriction on the rights of Indians. The time had come for a full-scale, nationwide Satyagraha campaign. Here, however, until someone was arrested for sedition, Satyagraha would have to be undertaken in a less direct manner. The approach he chose for the first stage was a national day of prayer and fasting and a one-day work-stoppage. The strike, which closed down all India for a day, signalled to the British the extent of Gandhi's influence. However, with so many people involved, not all of them committed to non-violence, the inevitable happened. Violence broke out and continued for several days, particularly in some of the remote provinces. As a result, Gandhi called off the effort admitting that "In the name of Satyagraha we have burnt down buildings, forcibly captured weapons, extorted money, stopped trains, cut off telegraph wires, killed innocent people, and plundered shops and private houses."[11] This event was the first indication of a truth he later acknowledged: Satyagraha was a life-changing proposition that might not always be an effective political tool with the masses. These setbacks however did not cause Gandhi to give upon Satyagraha as an effective tool for mass protest. Rather, he saw the need to develop a strategy that would capture the hearts of the people and their oppressors.

Eventually, Gandhi was arrested and imprisoned. It was in 1930, five years after his release from jail, that he implemented the most famous of all his Saytyagraha campaigns, the Salt March. Gandhi wrote a long letter to the viceroy specifying his demands, one of which was that the salt laws be abolished. Gandhi advised the viceroy that if all of his demands were not met he and his followers would disregard the salt laws. Gandhi saw these laws as highly symbolic of British exploitation. These laws prohibited the peasants from using local salt, and required them to purchase their salt from the British government's monopoly.

When the viceroy denied his request Gandhi began the famous Salt March. He and seventy-eight others marched from Sabamarti two hundred and forty miles to Dandi on the Indian seacoast. Upon reaching the seacoast, Gandhi unlawfully scooped up salt left from evaporated sea water. As thousands began to follow his lead by making their own salt or scooping it up from the beaches, the government responded with mass arrests eventually totalling 60,000. Gandhi also led a boycott of foreign cloth which became almost universal. The protests grew. Many quit government jobs and more refused to pay taxes. Gandhi was arrested and held for eight months without trial. While he was in jail the Satyagraha continued. This time the resisters seemed committed to his creed of nonviolence.

The turning point of the campaign was the march on the Dansa Salt Works. The world watched in horror as 2,000 unarmed Indians were bludgeoned, some to their death, by British soldiers. The Indians made no effort to fend off the blows as they marched by. In other parts of India protesters stood firm in their nonviolence in the face of machine-gun fire, and still others did not react violently when they were attacked by the police as they marched through the streets. Faced with an inability to maintain law and order and a significant drop in revenues, the government reached an agreement with Gandhi. They released him and eliminated the ban on making salt at home. They also agreed to release all nonviolent prisoners, to recognize the boycott of foreign cloth as a legitimate right, and to restore all confiscated property (taken by the government from those who refused to pay taxes). Gandhi explained his acceptance of terms short of self-government by stating another principle of Satyagraha: "There comes a time when the Satyagrahi may no longer refuse to negotiate with his opponent. His object is always to convert his opponent by love."[12] Negotiation to Gandhi did not mean abandonment of the goal of independence.

**A Return to Violence.** World War II put India in a unique situation with regard to Britain. Initially, Gandhi refused to authorize mass disobedience to gain independence, but the British continued to refuse to cooperate with the nationalists.

Gandhi compromised his position and declared open, non-violent rebellion. He was promptly arrested, and the masses revolted. Violence was widespread. He tried fasting to control the violence, but was not really successful.

The violence intensified after independence was granted. The Moslem and Hindu practitioners of Satyagraha who had held their ground so nobly and nonviolently against the British were intent on destroying each other. Events proved that Gandhi was correct when he preached that love of truth, love for all men, nonviolence, and unconcern for one's material position were essential to effective Satyagraha. The masses had not been converted to nonviolence as a way of life. Instead, as Gandhi had once stated, "mass civil disobedience may be and often is selfish in the sense that individuals expect personal gain from their disobedience."[13] The Moslem-Hindu violence that ultimately resulted in Gandhi's assassination was aflame in people who had practiced nonviolence as a last resort but without the essential commitment to truth and love.

**Gandhi's Influence.** These incidents reveal the development of his philosophy of nonviolence from a politically expedient means of redressing manifest wrongs to an entire way of life. His philosophy and methodology have influenced many who have felt the calling to obey a higher law. In fact, he had considerable influence on Martin Luther King's thinking.

As I delved deeper into the philosophy of Gandhi I came to see for the first time its potency in the area of social reform. Prior to reading Gandhi, I had about concluded that the ethics of Jesus were only effective in individual relationships. The turn the other cheek philosophy and the love your enemies philosophy were only valid, I felt, when individuals were in conflict with other individuals; when racial groups and nations were in conflict a more realistic approach seemed necessary. But after reading Gandhi, I saw how utterly mistaken I was. Gandhi was probably the first person in history to lift the love ethic of Jesus above mere interaction between individuals to a powerful and effective social force on a large scale.[14]

Gandhi-inspired nonviolence has occurred in countries under totalitarian regimes. While no such system has been overthrown, nonviolent resistance more often than not has had some effect. For example, Gandhi's influence was felt in Norway during the Nazi occupation in World War II. The Norwegian people's refusal to cooperate thwarted the Nazi effort to establish a puppet state there. The heroism of the Norwegian teachers in refusing to indoctrinate their pupils with Nazi ideology and to become part of the fascist teachers' corporation is perhaps the best-known part of this resistance.

The Sojourners Fellowship has adopted a Gandhian methodology in their Witness for Peace campaign opposing United States military involvement in Nicaragua. They have sent many people to Nicaragua to interfere with U.S. policy and to seek to change it. According to a recent article in *Sojourners*, "The idea, first proposed by Gandhi, of a peace army—a non-violent force of trained, disciplined and religious people ready to go to situations of conflict in order to make peace—is again causing great interest among many."[15]

Gandhi has not been without his critics. Pacifists have criticized him because of his attempt to apply nonviolence in a mass political struggle. He seemed to them dangerous because he accepted the need for confrontation and conflict. They also felt that he erred when he stated that violence was preferred to cowardice. Others have criticized him for trying to mobilize the masses to nonviolence when they did not share in his total philosophy. The situations where Gandhi lost control of the masses illustrate that this criticism is valid. Still others, who admitted the effectiveness of his methods against civilized powers, questioned their effectiveness against tyrants.

From Gandhi's experiences we can distill several important principles. As Christians—who are commanded to resist evil with good, love our enemies, and be subject to the powers and authorities that govern us—we should pay particular attention to these principles. The first is that a "manifest" wrong, such as discrimination or exploitation, must exist. Once the wrong is specifically identified, one should attempt by lawful means to eliminate the evil. If this fails, one should determine what means to pursue in opposing it. According to Gandhi's words and practice, one should probably pursue more lawful means of protest first. If these fail, then one should consider civil disobedience. Before engaging in any civil disobedience or protest, the evil and the method for opposing it must be communicated to the opponent. However, one is never to act when the opponent is unduly vulnerable. Besides being committed to nonviolence, the actors should expect suffering and retribution and submit to them. As Christians, we have been told to expect persecution for our beliefs and values; this last principle should come as no surprise to believers.

Gandhi concluded that the requirement that one love the adversary meant that one should be willing to negotiate. This too would seem to apply to Christians in most circumstances, except perhaps where the absolute right to worship is threatened. Also important is the fact that Gandhi generally had the support of the Indian people and the Indian National Congress to confirm his notion that an injustice had occurred. Gandhi, however, because of his position, was often able to act unilaterally. As Christians, we too should seek the support of the body before acting. We should always be examining our motives to ensure that we are not acting unilaterally.

We must also be wary of stopping with Gandhi. While no one doubts that Gandhi's contribution to the practice of civil disobedience was significant, he did not claim finality for his methods.

## Martin Luther King

In 1983 President Ronald Reagan signed into law legislation proclaiming Martin Luther King's birthday a national holiday. By joining the ranks of two of this country's greatest liberators, Washington and Lincoln, King has been immortalized as the leader of black people in their campaign for civil rights. Yet unlike Lincoln and Washington, King was arrested over thirty times. His name is linked not to making law, but to breaking it.

**Development of a Philosophy: Christianity and Gandhism Meet.** King's prominence as a civil rights leader often obscures that of his earlier calling as a Baptist preacher. But it is the "preacher" which is evident in the passion, the earnestness, the compassion for his fellow human being, and his philosophy of nonviolent action. His philosophy was part Christian, part Gandhian, and in part hammered out in his own experience. As King was fond of saying, "Christ furnished the spirit and motivation [for his movement] and Gandhi furnished the method."[16]

As a student at Morehouse College in Atlanta, King read Thoreau's essay on civil disobedience and was fascinated by the idea of refusing to cooperate with an evil system. According to King, this was his first intellectual contact with the theory of nonviolent resistance. In seminary, he read Gandhi's works, and they revolutionized his thinking regarding the Christian principles of turning the other cheek and loving one's enemies. To King, Gandhi applied these principles beyond individuals and initiated a powerful social force on a large scale. By the time King ended his formal education he held the conviction "that nonviolent resistance was one of the most potent weapons available for people in their quest for social justice."[17]

King's philosophy was most commonly expressed in terms of Christian love. One writer has suggested that "King's genius—and it was that precisely—was not in the application of Gandhism to the Negro struggle but in the transmuting of Gandhism by grafting it onto the only thing that could give it relevance and force in the Negro community, the Negro religious tradition."[18] As a Baptist preacher, King was a firm believer in the redemptive power of Christ and that the Christian call was to overcome evil with good. Because Southern black preachers in the 1950s and 1960s were often leaders in their communities, King's position as pastor of the Dexter Avenue Baptist Church gave him a platform from which to express his views. Through his sermons he identified the basis of the wrongs to be redressed and the attitudes, outlook, and means necessary to redress them. His sermons revealed that his beliefs were at the heart of his actions.

Love and forgiveness were the attitudes that blacks were to have towards their white brothers. To King the lesson of Calvary was that goodness drives out evil and only love can conquer hate. Thus, love was the only force that was capable of transforming an enemy into a friend. King noted that by loving one's enemies one recognizes his unique relationship to God. As a result of this love one is also to have a forgiving attitude towards the oppressor. Just as Christ forgave those who crucified him, because they knew not what they did, King preached that blacks were to forgive those who persecuted them out of moral blindness. Because of this blindness, many Christians engaged in misguided actions. Moral blindness was the result of years of rationalizations which had clothed obvious wrongs in the "garments of righteousness." Blacks, like Christ, were to forgive this blindness.

King also insisted that Paul's command to "be not conformed to this world, but be transformed by a renewing of your mind" gave Christians a mandate for nonconformity. As Christians, they were to live differently, according to a higher loyalty. Most people, and Christians in particular, "are thermometers that record or register the temperature of majority opinion, not thermostats that transform and regulate the temperature of society." According to King, the church, including the black church, had too long condoned the immoral and unethical. To his relatively affluent black congregation at Dexter Avenue he proclaimed that "we need to recapture the gospel glow of the early Christians who were nonconformists in the truest sense of the word and refused to shape their witness according to the mundane patterns of the world. Willingly they sacrificed fame, fortune, and life itself in behalf of a cause they knew to be right." Thus to be a noncomformist was costly. He told them that they must be neighbors to one another and to their white brother, that white Christians must learn to be neighbors too and that the "true neighbor must risk his position, his prestige, and even his life for the welfare of others."[19]

In addition to being nonconformists, King counselled being wise as serpents and harmless as doves, or being tough-minded and tenderhearted. In order to end segregation, there was a need for people with wisdom—tough minds characterized by incisive thinking, realistic appraisal, and decisive judgment. Yet they were to be tenderhearted as well. King taught that bringing together tough-mindedness and tender-heartedness was required if blacks were to move creatively toward the goal of freedom and justice.

This creativity was to be expressed in the form of nonviolent resistance. Violence, said King, "brings only temporary victories; violence by creating many more social problems than it solves, never brings permanent peace."[20] Rather, through nonviolence they could resist the unjust system and at the same time love the perpetrators of the system. One's *means* of ending an injustice were to be as pure as the *ends*. "For in the long run we must see that the means represent the end in process and the ideal in the making."[21]

Like Gandhi, King saw these means as including redemptive suffering:

We shall match your capacity to inflict suffering by our capacity to endure suffering. We shall meet your physical force with soul force. Do to us what you will we will continue to love you. We cannot in good conscience obey your unjust laws, because non-cooperation with evil is as much a moral obligation as cooperation with good. Throw us in jail and we will still love you. Send your hooded perpetrators of violence into our communities at midnight and beat us and leave us half dead and we shall still love you. But be ye assured that we will wear you down by our capacity to suffer. One day we shall win freedom, but not only for ourselves, we shall so appeal to your heart and conscience that we shall win you in the process and our victory will be a double victory.[22]

For resistance to be successful one's adversaries should be converted.

By advocating nonviolent resistance as the means of accomplishing goals, King insisted that he was not taking things into his own hands because God was not able. God was indeed able to, and does, subdue the powers of evil. But human beings need not necessarily wait submissively, doing nothing and expecting God to alleviate all suffering. As Christians, King advocated that people not only pray "with unceasing passion for social justice," but also use their "minds to develop a program, organize [them]selves into mass nonviolent action and employ every resource of [their] bodies and souls to bring an end to racial injustice."[23] To King, prayer was not a substitute for intelligence and hard work.

King recognized that methods of nonviolent resistance sometimes included acts of civil disobedience. He was often accused of being inconsistent because of his insistence on lawfulness while advocating civil disobedience. His response echoes Aquinas in part and Gandhi in part. King defended his position in his "Letter From a Birmingham Jail" explaining that

There are two types of laws; just and unjust. I would be the first to advocate obeying just laws. One has not only a legal but a moral responsibility to obey just laws. Conversely, one has a moral responsibility to disobey unjust laws. I would agree with St. Augustine that "an unjust law is no law at all."

... A just law is a man-made code that squares with the moral law or the law of God. An unjust law is a code that is out of harmony with the moral. To put it in the terms of St. Thomas Aquinas: "An unjust law is a human law that is not rooted in eternal law and natural law. . . ."

... An unjust law is a code that a numerical or power majority group compels a minority group to obey but does not make binding on itself. . . a just law is a code that a majority compels a minority to follow and that it is willing to follow itself. . . .

... A law is unjust if it is inflicted on a minority that, as a result of being denied the right to vote, had no part in enacting or devising the law. . . .

... In no sense do I advocate evading or defying the law as would the rabid segregationist. That would lead to anarchy. One who breaks an unjust law must do so openly, lovingly, and with a willingness to accept the penalty . . . to arouse the conscience of the community over its injustice, is in reality expressing the highest respect for the law.[24]

Initially, civil disobedience was not prominent in the civil rights struggle. Those laws that were violated were local ordinances or state laws which, according to King, contradicted national law and constitutional rights. The direct action served to expose the "illegality" of the local law.

**The Montgomery Story: King's Philosophy in Practice.** King's first encounter with nonviolent resistance was the now famous boycott in Montgomery, Alabama. In 1953, the Supreme Court had overruled the 1896 *Plessy* v. *Ferguson* decision, which held that the provision of separate but equal facilities to blacks was not unconstitutional. Yet the state of Alabama had segregation laws which applied to buses. In Montgomery, these statutes were applied in order to restrict blacks to the back of the bus even if the "white" seats were empty, and to require that they stand if all the seats allotted to white people were occupied and a white person entered the bus. If the blacks refused to stand and move back they were subject to arrest. But, on December 1, 1955, Rosa Parks refused to move to the back of the bus, and the civil rights movement shifted into high gear.

The decision to boycott the bus company was made at a meeting of civic and religious leaders. They opened the meeting with prayer and with a devotional period. At a later mass meeting, also begun with prayer and reading of the scriptures, King emphasized that, as Christians, the boycotters were to love their enemies and to pray for those that persecuted them. A resolution was adopted declaring that the boycott would continue until courteous treatment by the bus operators was guaranteed, passengers were seated on a first-come-first-served basis with blacks towards the back and whites towards the front, and Negro bus operators were employed on predominantly Negro routes.

Though the protests were moderate and nonviolent, with continual emphasis on loving enemies and neighbors, the white community resisted concessions. King's home and the homes of other black ministers involved in the movement were bombed. The Montgomery Improvement Association (MIA), organizer of the protest, was required to move its headquarters several times due to alleged zoning violations. The black-owned taxi companies who had assisted in providing transportation were reminded of a statute that required them to charge a minimum fare of forty cents. The MIA responded by organizing a massive city-wide car pool system. Policemen began arresting people waiting for rides on charges of vagrancy and loitering. Several participants in the boycott, including King, were arrested for violating the state's antiboycott law and found guilty on March 19, 1956. From this point onward the bus boycott was no longer a protest, it was civil disobedience. Despite these setbacks, the boycott continued nonviolently.

Like Gandhi, King was willing to use the courts to redress wrongs. Therefore, the MIA had filed suit in federal district court asking for the end of bus segregation on the grounds that it violated the Fourteenth Amendment to the United States Constitution. King realized that, while the courts could not change hearts, they could alter habits. He said "let us never succumb to the temptation of believing that legislation and judicial decrees play only minor roles in solving this problem. Morality cannot be legislated but behavior can be regulated. Judicial decrees may not change the heart, but they can restrain the heartless."[25]

On June 4, 1956, the federal district court held bus segregation unconstitutional. Undaunted, the city immediately appealed the decision to the Supreme Court and began to initiate proceedings challenging the legality of the alternate transportation system set up by the MIA. On November 13, 1956, almost one year from the boycott's beginning, during a hearing on the legality of the transportation system set up by the MIA, the Supreme Court affirmed the judgment of the federal district court declaring the segregation system unconstitutional. One bystander echoed the sentiments of the crowd in saying, "God Almighty has spoken (through the Supreme Court) from Washington, D.C."

Once desegregation was to take place, King and his group developed a publicity campaign complete with instruction advocating nonviolent resistance and courtesy when they began to ride the buses again. The training included role playing of potential scenes where blacks were harassed by white passengers or bus drivers. In each case a nonviolent response was provided by the insulted passenger. Many feel that this effort was a significant factor in the relative peace that followed.

While the battle for desegregation was not over in Montgomery, the Supreme Court's decision marked the beginning of the end. It also signalled victory for King's nonviolent approach. Nonviolence was slow, however. It had been a painful year. Nor was it successful by itself; the Supreme Court's decision was the factor that finally forced the city's hand. However, the protest succeeded in focusing national attention on the plight of the Negro and in engaging the national conscience on their side. King learned that publicity, and a flair for the dramatic could influence public opinion nationwide. This was a lesson he never forgot. While nonviolent resistance might not convert one's immediate oppressor, it could stimulate public opinion and force the powers that be to bring about change. Thus, King often referred to his experience in Montgomery as having done more to clarify his thinking regarding nonviolence than the books he had read.

**Beyond Montgomery.** King's next major civil rights demonstration, the Prayer Pilgrimage of May 17, 1957, was the largest civil rights demonstration yet organized. It brought 35,000 people from thirty states to the Lincoln Memorial to pray for equal rights and an end to the injustices. The Pilgrimage launched King into a position of leadership and united much of the black population behind him. From this posture he could begin to branch out and affect segregation policies across the country.

When Negro students began sit-ins at segregated lunch counters, restaurants, department stores, and libraries, King was quick to recognize that such actions constituted the next phase of the movement. He also sensed that if sit-ins became violent they could be counter-productive. Convinced that they would quickly die out without organization, he and the Southern Christian Leadership Conference, of which he was head, organized a student conference to evolve a strategy for the sit-ins. While King encouraged the students to "delve deeper into the philosophy of nonviolence," they tended to view it as a political tactic promising certain results. Consequently, the group which came out of this meeting, the Student Nonviolent Coordinating Committee (SNCC), tended to maintain a more militant posture than did King.

The same philosophy was applied in the Freedom Rides of which King served as spokesman. Although committed to nonviolence, King was aware that the rides might well provoke violence. He told the riders in training sessions that they "must develop the quiet courage of dying for a cause. We would not like to see anyone die. We all love life and there are no martyrs here—but we are all aware that we may have some casualties." King was criticized for his involvement with the freedom rides by both white liberals and blacks who felt that the rides were not practical and were too provocative. However, King insisted that the undesirable and often violent reaction to the riders was the "creative tension" necessary to the birth of a new order. King seemed willing to exploit the use of violence by the adversary to catch the public eye. The freedom rides and later incidents reveal King's willingness to consider the "media worthiness" of his alternatives.

King encountered his first setback in Albany, Georgia. The Albany community reacted peacefully to the campaign, rendering it largely unsuccessful. The local sheriff arrested the demonstrators for unlawful assembly and disturbing the peace. Television viewers were not as appalled as they were when freedom riders were physically abused by segregationist groups.

Too much dramatic publicity could lead to bizarre results, however. In Birmingham in 1963, he decided to have "children's only" marches. On May 2, 1963, about 1,000 children marched from the Sixteenth Street Baptist Church towards downtown Birmingham. Nearly 1,000 were arrested. The next day, even more children marched and the Birmingham police responded with high-powered fire hoses, sticks, and dogs. The news media photographed children being bowled over with the hoses and being bitten by police dogs. Public opinion was outraged. A *New York Times* editorial commented that the Birmingham "barbarities" were "revoltingly reminiscent of totalitarian excesses."

It worked! With jails filled to capacity and the city on the brink of total social disorder, the city agreed to negotiate with King and other black leaders. With the white community's back to the wall King could negotiate from a position of strength. The city officials agreed to desegregate lunch counters, restrooms, fitting rooms, and drinking fountains; to release the demonstrators on nominal bonds; and to adopt fair hiring practices. The march seemed a complete success.

Or was it? After the settlement was announced, segregationists reacted by bombing King's hotel and his brother's home. The black community responded with riots. Cars were destroyed, property was burned, and policemen and civilians were injured. Like Gandhi, King had to go through the city to calm things down. In a sense, the riot was a defeat for his nonviolent approach. However, most of the rioters were not active members of the Birmingham protest group, and the riot would have probably been worse had it not been for King's emphasis on nonviolence throughout the protest.

The campaign is also remembered for King's famous "Letter from a Birmingham Jail" in which he explained his reasons for being in Birmingham and for disobeying a court order barring mass marches, boycotts, and sit-ins. He and his followers had marched despite this order and King had been jailed. Many had criticized his timing of the campaign and argued that he would have been better off to wait. In the "Letter" he defends his timing, saying that he had "never yet engaged in a direct action movement that was 'well-timed' according to those who have not suffered unduly from the disease of segregation. . . . 'justice too long delayed is justice denied.' We have waited more than three hundred and forty years for our constitutional and God-given rights."[26] He explained that direct action and disobedience were not alternatives to negotiation but were designed to create the tension necessary to force negotiation from a community which had heretofore refused to do so. He differentiated between nonviolent tension and violent tension. He said, "We must see the need of having nonviolent gadflies to create the kind of tension in a society that will help men to rise from the dark depths of prejudice and racism."

Was he an extremist as some accused? His "Letter" responded: "If our white brothers dismiss as 'rabble rousers' and 'outside agitators' those of us working through channels of nonviolent direct action, and refuse to support our nonviolent efforts, millions of Negroes, out of frustration and despair will seek solace and security in black nationalist ideologies which will lead to an inevitably frightening racial nightmare."[27] There was even some satisfaction in being considered an extremist: "Was not Jesus an extremist in love 'Love your enemies, bless them that curse you, pray for them that despitefully use you.'"

Perhaps the civil rights movement and King's approach reached its climax in the historic march on Washington where some 250,000 people gathered for the largest civil rights demonstration to date. There King delivered his stirring "I Have a Dream" speech. Uplifted and encouraged, the black community seemed united and ready to follow King nonviolently to the finish. This unity was shortlived. Just eighteen days later, four girls were killed when a Sunday school class in a black church in Birmingham was bombed. Blacks from all sectors were demanding open, all-out civil disobedience. King, feeling that the time was not right for full-scale civil disobedience, refused to lead the rebellion that followed. He was severely criticized for not leading what he had started.

In many ways, 1964 was both the brightest and the darkest hour of the civil rights movement. On July 2, 1964, the Civil Rights Act was passed, symbolizing the federal government's commitment to the plight of black Americans. King had actively urged it on both President Kennedy, who introduced the bill, and President Johnson, who pressured the Congress until it was passed. The act was significant because it gave the movement another means of enforcing rights.

Also in 1964, King was awarded the Nobel Peace Prize for keeping his followers to the principle of nonviolence. "Without King's confirmed effectiveness . . . demonstrations and marches could easily have become violent and ended with the spilling of blood."[28]

Yet, 1964 was also the darkest hour. It was the year that, for a time, King lost control of the movement. Riots and violence terrorized communities, towns, and even the nation's largest cities during the summer of that year. There was an ever-widening gulf between the SCLC, headed by King, and the SNCC and other more radical black groups. In many of these other groups, nonviolence had become a bad word.

With these accomplishments and others like the Selma march in the area of civil rights, King began to focus his nonviolent tactics on what he perceived to be the two other looming injustices remaining in the United States. One was the Vietnam War. To King, it was worthless to discuss integration if there was no world to integrate into. He felt that the nonviolence he preached was inconsistent with the violence of the war: "I knew that I could never again raise my voice against the violence of the oppressed in the ghettos without having spoken clearly to the greatest purveyor of violence in the world today—my own country."[29] As with the civil rights movement, he began to lead marches protesting the war and to organize workers to spread opposition to the war.

The second injustice was poverty. As racial riots continued and nonviolence became history, King decided that the solution to the problem would have to be economic. He decided to organize a poor people's march on Washington to dramatize the plight of the poor of all complexions. King's proposed march garnered support from the violent black power wing. However, before he would agree to their participation, he stated that they all would have to pledge themselves to nonviolence. King never led the march. While in Memphis, where there was racial unrest due to a black garbagemen's strike, he was assassinated.

**King, Similar to Gandhi, Yet Different.** It is ironic, yet perhaps indicative of the evil in the world, that the two men in this century most committed to nonviolence died violent deaths. Both King and Gandhi sought to lift their people out from under the oppression of an unsympathetic government. Both were largely successful, yet both, despite their insistence on nonviolence, generated movements which often resulted in acts of violence, either by the oppressor or by the oppressed. However, because of their commitment to direct confrontation with the oppressor, neither were pacifists in the true sense of the term.

King's methodology in Montgomery was similar to Gandhi's but had its own unique features. Unlike Gandhi, he never felt compelled to warn his adversaries or to notify the authorities of grievances or plans for nonviolent action. On the contrary, in many cases secrecy was stressed. Also unlike Gandhi, King usually did not serve his jail sentences, paying fines to get out. In at least one instance, local officials, not wanting to make a martyr of King by jailing him, paid the fine themselves. While King seemed to adopt nonviolence as a philosophy of life, he was never so concerned as Gandhi that his followers do so. He realized that most people in Montgomery did not believe in nonviolence as he did, but because it was presented to them as Christianity in action, they were willing to adopt it as a technique. He viewed their willingness to use nonviolence as a technique as a step forward, and the person who went this far was more likely to adopt nonviolence as a way of life.

But, like Gandhi, he repeatedly stressed these elements of nonviolent resistance: that it is not for cowards, that it does not seek to humiliate one's opponents, that it is directed against the forces of evil, that it suffers without retaliation, that it avoids internal violence, and that the universe is on the side of justice. Furthermore, like Gandhi, he recognized that preparation was important before nonviolence could be effective. For example, participants in the Birmingham protest were asked to fill out a pledge entitled "Commandments for the Volunteers." Volunteers signing the pledge committed themselves to the nonviolent movement and agreed to keep these "Ten Commandments."[30]

1. Meditate daily on the teachings and life of Jesus.

2. Remember always that the nonviolent movement in Birmingham seeks justice and reconciliation—not a victory.

3. Walk and talk in the manner of love for God is Love.

4. Pray daily to be used by God in order that all men might be free.

5. Sacrifice personal wishes in order that all men might be free.

6. Observe with both friend and foe the ordinary rules of courtesy.

7. Seek to perform regular service for others and for the world.

8. Refrain from violence of fist, tongue or heart.

9. Strive to be in good spiritual and bodily health.

10. Follow the directions of the movement and of the captain on the demonstration.

Also like Gandhi, King's role was often that of firefighter. Many groups engaging in protest would start out peacefully. However, the situations would often become explosive and violence would break out on both sides. King would rush in to calm the blacks and negotiate with the whites. When things got out of hand in India it was Gandhi, through his speaking or more often his fasting, that would calm the masses.

**Application of King's Principles to Christian Action.** Just as Gandhi's methodology of protest applies to Christians seeking to oppose injustices so does King's. The starting point of King's philosophy and that of all Christians is that Christ commands us to love our enemies. Once that principle is acknowledged, the emphasis shifts to the injustice—what it is and how to remedy it. Unlike Thoreau and Gandhi, King always seemed to have a structure within which to make such decisions. In Montgomery it was the MIA, afterwards it was the SCLC. While King exercised a great deal of control over these groups, they were not necessarily composed of "yes-men." In this way, he was able to consider the views of other Christians and had a means of confirming his decisions. Whether this mechanism always produced sound and godly plans is a matter of debate. Yet it did seem to prevent King from acting unilaterally.

As far as his actual strategy is concerned, there are several things that we as Christians should consider. Unlike Gandhi, who laid out his grievances and his plans to the opposition before embarking on a nonviolent campaign, King did not generally do so. He preferred to initiate a program with an element of surprise. Even in Birmingham, where he clearly announced the campaign, he kept the details secret. In this sense, he was more of a pragmatist than Gandhi, who seemed constrained by the ideal.

King's resistance, especially in later years, was basically a three-pronged attack. The first was mass nonviolent action on the local level. Frequent meetings were held to inform the participants of Christ's teachings on loving one's enemies. Training sessions were held to develop proper responses among the people. They were advised that they must be willing to suffer physically and mentally. King emphasized that as Christians they were to expect it and were to face it as Christ would have. His emphasis on both the centrality of Christ and the practical equipping for witness ought to commend itself to Christians.

During the protest, King would often have the NAACP file lawsuits seeking the redress of the grievances involved. In Montgomery, in St. Augustine, and in Selma, the courts held favorably to his cause. While he never appeared to base this action on scriptural principles, clearly such action would be appropriate for Christians in light of the Romans 13 requirement that respect be accorded governing authorities.

King would also engage in direct petition to the federal government. This practice met with success in the form of the Civil Rights Act. Again respect for the governing authorities would seem to require such action on the part of Christians.

Lastly, like Gandhi, King emphasized that the end of a protest was to convert the oppressors. Again, this view is consistent with a Christian perspective. However, King's more pragmatic side often stated that the goal of a given campaign was to create tension to force negotiation. While this goal may seem inconsistent with the stated end of a protest, it need not be. To convert one's opponent, one must have dialogue. To the extent that creating tension produces this dialogue it is consistent with the goal to convert the other side. The danger, however, was that in getting the publicity necessary to create the tension, King may have sacrificed the means for the ends. For example, sending small children out to demonstrate in Birmingham when it was fairly certain that they would be arrested or assaulted may have been "brilliant" in terms of attracting the public's attention, but it was questionable as a legitimate means of Christian nonviolent protest. Thus, the Christian must always be asking if the means used are a positive witness to the state and if they are consistent with the ends.

# SIX

# Holy Disobedience:
# A Christian Tradition

THE "CLOUD OF WITNESSES" across space and time is united in its radical declaration that Jesus is Lord. It is universal in its proclamation that a new order has come—an order which both now is, and is to come. Its vision is of the consummation of history—a new heaven and a new earth and the judgment of this world.

However, the cloud dissipates into a fog as soon as the question is asked concerning just how these convictions shape the believer's relationship to society, culture, government, and law. In his near-classic study, *Christ and Culture*, H. Richard Niebuhr calls the relationship of Christianity and culture an "enduring and perennial problem" which has yielded no single answer: "So many voices are heard, so many confident but diverse assertions about the Christian answer . . . that bewilderment and uncertainty beset many Christians."[1]

The issue of the authority of the state and the duty of obedience or submission to it is a substantial aspect of the larger issue of the Christian's relationship to society and culture. Especially in a day when law has expanded to include so much of our cultural vision ("public policy"), it is clear that law is both a response to, and a creation of, culture. Our theology of the world and our sense of our relationship to history will shape our understanding of law and our duties and rights toward it.

To explore the varieties of tradition—both action and analysis, theology and praxis—is not merely to engage in a historical inquiry. It is rather to seek the counsel of the saints, the discernment of the body, the witness of the community. The issues raised in Louisville, Moscow, or Krakow are not novel. The inquiries into the application of Romans 13, the meaning of "just law," and the competing claims of Christ and Caesar are recurring. We fail our community if we do not both listen to its teaching and witness its faithfulness.

History discovers a multitude of voices; some may perceive a choir, others a cacophony. But we shall also likely perceive a church whose teachings were shaped not only by the sharp two-edged sword of scripture, but by the anvil of history. Good theology has always spoken to, and emerged from, the experience of God's people. This was true in biblical days of slavery, exodus, captivity, and restoration. The experiences of fleeing the Egyptians, facing the Philistines, and suffering under the Babylonians produced the faith. Similarly, the church collectively and believers individually have rarely developed their theology of culture and law under the shelter of the university. It has been shaped by the experiences of a Diocletian and a Constantine, of catacombs and cathedrals. The history of Christ's church has produced the works of Augustine, Aquinas, Calvin, and Menno Simons.

The task of the faithful has always been, and still is, to take our experience—including our culture, conscience, community—and read it in the light of our biblical faith. So it is that theology shapes experience and experience theology. Our doctrine of sovereignty, our conception of the State, even (perhaps especially) our eschatology will impact our interpretation of the current situation and shape our response.

The dimensions of our Christian heritage are vast and complex, the hues and shadows subtle. They are beyond our present scope, and perhaps our expertise. But a review of some of the prominent personalities and the movements they fostered is essential.

## The Early Church to Constantine

Until the legalization of Christianity by Constantine in 313 A.D., the faithful frequently found themselves clashing with the Roman government and Roman culture. While Rome could find room for many religions, its very culture, Gibbon notes, required a sort of "live and let live" style among competing religious traditions. But radical monotheism, as in Christianity, was something else. Thus, Gibbon insists that it was to be "expected that they [the Romans] would unite with indignation against any sect of people which should separate itself from the communion of mankind and claim the exclusive possession of divine knowledge [and] should disdain every form of worship except its own as impious and idolatrous."[2] As H. Richard Niebuhr observes, the conviction of the ultimate claims of God not only hedges kings, but all symbols of political power: "monotheism deprives them of their sacred aura."[3] Thus, in spite of affirmations about the legitimacy of government and a non-political agenda, the fundamental clash between Christ and Roman culture was perhaps inherent and inescapable. Ernest Troeltsch observed the "curious blend of conservative and revolutionary elements" in the early Christians' teachings, but argued that in spite of the conservative elements, Christianity contained "immense spiritual energies of a revolutionary nature" and that even when it tolerated an existing order, "inwardly it undermined it."[4] Thus, persecution seemed inevitable.

While the widespread persecutions of the Christians did not take place until the middle of the second century, the very fact of Paul's imprisonment and the activities of the infamous Nero in 54 A.D. are evidence of earlier persecution. In 202 A.D. an edict forbidding conversions to Christianity was issued by Septimus Severus. While, in theory, this edict did not punish the existing Christians, it did place them in direct conflict with the government since witnessing to the Lord would be encouraging others to civil disobedience. In 249 A.D., the Emperor Decius ordered all citizens to sacrifice to the Roman gods. This edict led to the persecution and death of many Christians who refused to obey it. Perhaps the most egregious edict was issued by the Emperor Valerian in 257 A.D., subjecting Christians to the death penalty if they so much as went to any church meetings or services. In addition, the early Christians were obviously offended by the "cult of the Emperor" which faced them at every turn, requiring sacrifice to and reverence of the emperors as gods.

As further decrees against Christianity were issued, early Christians had to choose between obeying the government and abandoning their faith or suffering for their beliefs. Early church fathers were forced to assess the legitimacy of a government which compelled them to do what God prohibited. The arguments were framed in higher-law terms. A North African Christian, Tertullian (160 A.D.-230 A.D.), sought to convince the authorities that Christians should be accorded religious freedom: "If you [the Roman government] are saying that Christianity is illegal simply because that is your will, not because it really ought to be illegal.... If a law of yours has erred it is, I presume, because it was conceived by man; it certainly did not fall from heaven." Romans 13 did not mean that all laws and all exercises of authority by the government were proper; rather, law was justified only if it prohibited what was evil and justified what was good.

Origen, one of the greatest thinkers in the early church, concurred: "One may only obey the laws of the state when they agree with Divine law; when however, the written law of the state commands something other than the Divine and Natural law, then we must ignore the commands of the State and obey the commands of God alone."

Irenaeus viewed the state in a more positive light, teaching that government was instituted as a remedy for sin. Irenaeus is believed to have suffered a martyr's death. It is likely, therefore, that he believed that the secular authority could abuse its divine mandate, though the principle of secular authority was a divine one. The "prophet" Hermas went even further, contrasting the laws of the City of God with the city of this world: "Wilt thou on account of thy fields and of thy property, abjure thy law and live according to the law of this city? See thou that it be not thy ruin to deny thy law.... Since thou art dwelling in a foreign land."

Nonetheless, Origen, Tertullian, Irenaeus, and Hermas recognized the value of the *pax Romana* and the social order to the spreading of the gospel. They realized that God used evil, godless men for the ordering of the whole. It was the Roman idolatry and opposition to Christianity to which these writers addressed themselves, rather than the legitimacy of the Roman government itself. Their resistance was limited to refusals to worship the emperor or obey laws they believed contrary to the will of God. The only legitimate form of resistance was suffering and passive resistance. In all else they honored the government and the emperor as an authority appointed by God.

A discussion of civil disobedience in the first few centuries of the church would not be complete without looking at the views of the early church on soldiering and war. As sacrificing to the emperor became a required part of service in the imperial army, Paul's command to give "honor to whom honor is due" became a moral dilemma. This dilemma of conscience led to the emergence of resistant and pacifist thinking in the early church. The writings of these and later pacifists provide some of the richest and most thoughtful literature on civil disobedience.

However, the early Christians did not deal with the issue of pacifism to the extent that it involved the refusal to take part in war until the middle of the second century. Early Christians were largely peaceloving people and the Roman army did not resort to conscription.[5] However, after 170 A.D. references to Christian soldiers began to appear. The debate appeared to focus on two issues. Should the Christian disobey if ordered to join the Roman legions, and what was the duty of the man who was already a soldier when he converted to Christianity? Was he to "abide by the calling to which he was called" (1 Corinthians) or to quit the army, a clear case of desertion and a violation of Roman law.

In 298 A.D., a centurion known as Marcellus refused to remain in the army because of the requirements to sacrifice to gods and emperors. Since he had already achieved the rank of centurion, there is some support for the notion that many of the early Christians who refused to participate in the military did so because of the requirement that they engage in idolatrous practices rather than because of opposition to military service.[6] These Christians would obey government until asked to do something that denied God.

Some first- and second-century Christians were opposed to war in and of itself. Tertullian did not seem to think that a Christian could even be a soldier exempt from sacrifices: ". . . shall the son of peace take part in battle when it does not become him to sue at law?" Origen also wrote that "We no longer take up 'sword against nation,' nor do we 'learn war anymore' having become children of peace for the sake of Jesus who is our leader."

## Constantinian Settlement

In the fourth century, the Emperor Constantine was converted. Pagan religions were soon banned. Christians began exerting a greater role in the social order, assuming leadership in their communities and gaining social status. The papacy grew in power and began to exercise its influence in political circles. Some theologians view the Synod of Arles as the point at which the church, "in return for governmental protection," at last wholeheartedly accepted civil and military obligations. Was this a great victory for the Christian faith or the beginning of a tragedy—the secularization of the faith?

The clashes between civil and religious authority were not over, however. When, in 385, the Emperor Valentinian took steps to appropriate one of the churches for use by a heretical group, Ambrose garnered a great deal of public support and protested this move. Without bloodshed and violence, he prevailed. Some have called this the church's first exercise of passive resistance.[7] The new era, however, required a new analysis of church and state, Christ and culture, religion and government.

Probably the best-known Christian in the period immediately following Constantine's conversion is Ambrose's pupil, Augustine (354-430). Augustine's writing on the relationships between the state, the church, the individual, and evil are helpful in understanding how Christians of this period viewed obedience to government. *The City of God* is a classic statement of the relationship of faith to the worldly order.

Augustine saw the state as a necessary evil; once sin was in the world, social institutions were necessary to combat it. However, Augustine recognized that the state is not the widest society to which the individual Christian belongs, the Kingdom of God is.

Since government, although ordained by God, was the result of human sin, it was corruptible by that same sin. Unjust laws were possible and, according to Augustine, "an unjust law is no law at all." If the state commands something contrary to the laws of God's Kingdom the Christian should not obey, but Augustine did not advocate violence to achieve change. Rather he described the Christian as one "who prefers to endure evil so as not to commit it rather than to commit evil so as not to endure it." Unlike many early Christian writers, Augustine did not see killing as necessarily evil. In his view when a soldier kills an enemy or when a judge orders the execution of a criminal no sin occurs. The monarch has the responsibility of deciding whether another country should be punished for injustices it has committed. Thus, if the law requires military service in a just war it is a legitimate claim.

After Augustine's death, church teachings often seemed to elevate the authority of the secular rulers without regard to their adherence to divine or natural law. The notion that kings were given divine inspiration began to become popular. Pope Gregory I stated, "That those who murmur against the rulers set over them speak not against a human being, but against Him who disposes all things to divine order." Yet, Gregory himself imposed limits on this position when he disobeyed the imperial authorities by signing a separate truce with the invading Lombards. By the ninth century, the teachings of church fathers such as Augustine were again stressed. The feudal system emphasized a contractual relationship between the ruler and the ruled. In this situation the concept that legitimate authority was based on the fulfillment of certain duties developed. However, the idea that rulers were divinely inspired was still prevalent.

Certainly the most influential theologian of this era was Thomas Aquinas (1225-1274). The typical view of world order at this time was that Western Europe was Christendom, and that Christendom was divided into two arms. One arm was the church and the papacy and the other arm was the state and Holy Roman Emperor. The rulers were theoretically subject to church discipline, and as a result the clergy held significant political power. Struggles between the two were not seen as the church versus the state, but were viewed as a schism within the church. Theories of civil disobedience were based on the notion that rulers, though divinely ordained, could not rule based on whim, but were bound by the divine laws which must be observed by all. A tyrant could be slain. Between the eleventh and thirteenth centuries, the papacy used this argument to claim greater control over secular activities, and was resisted in this by secular rulers.

Aquinas saw the state not only as an instrument for restraining evil but also as a natural expression of human nature. Government had a positive role in furthering the purposes for which society existed. In the Thomistic view of government, sin "has no part in the rational justification of the state.... Man is unthinkable without the state because it is only in the state and through the state that he can achieve perfection." The purpose of the state is the maintenance of order and peace, the creation of a setting for the exercise of vocation, a minimal legal morality, and the ideal of justice. The state was "the preparatory school for the cultivation of a Christian disposition."[8]

Authority, essential in any community, comes from God, but God does not designate certain people to rule. The people have the right to designate who shall have authority and to remove it. For Aquinas, "Authority may fail to derive from God for two reasons: either because of the way in which it was obtained, or in consequence of the use which is made of it."

Law was the means by which God expressed his sovereignty on earth. The highest law is divine law, whose commandments are not subject to the imperfections of man's perception of law. Aquinas' perspective on human law became a major component of Christian tradition:

> Laws framed by man are either just or unjust. If they are just they have the power of binding in conscience, from the eternal law from which they are derived. . . . On the other hand laws may be unjust in two ways. First by being contrary to human good. . . . such laws do not bind the conscience, except perhaps in order to avoid scandal or disturbance, for which cause a just man should even yield his right.
>
> Secondly, laws may be unjust, through being opposed to the Divine good. Such are the laws of tyrants inducing to idolatry, or to anything contrary to the Divine law; and *laws of this kind must in no way be observed.*[9] (emphasis added)

John of Salisbury had claimed that a tyrant may be killed because he has violated the laws and customs of the country. Aquinas, sensitive to the importance of social order in Romans and the injustices that early Christians were enduring at the time of its writing, felt that the people should endure the tyrant unless he was outrageous. He counsels that no private citizen, but only public authority, should dispose of the tyrant. Such persons acting in their public character are not mere law-breakers, they are rather law-judgers, exercising the public function as representatives of the people.

Like Augustine, Aquinas viewed it entirely proper for Christians to take part in a just war. For a war to be just, it must be waged by a sovereign authority, when a grievous wrong has been committed, with the intention to promote good. A refusal to fight on religious grounds would probably have had little hope of transforming the king's policy and could expect severe punishment.[10]

From this period it seems that we can take two principles regarding civil disobedience. First, although rulers or the government might derive their authority from God and profess to be Christian, they might make unjust laws. If they did so, the Christian had a God-given right, sometimes even duty, to disobey. Second, when a government professes to be Christian and when Christians have a significant role in government, it is likely that much of what the government does will be viewed as just and proper by the church. The concrete influence of Christian leadership in a society may indeed encourage laws which legitimately deserve the support of the church, but the potential for seduction by the powers is always present. Where, as in this period, church and state are largely offices of one ideology, the potential for prophetic challenge is minimal.

## The Reformation

The sixteenth century saw the collapse of the medieval synthesis. A new order was developing in Europe which would have a profound impact on concepts of church and state, and thus on law. Indeed, the reformers took issue not only with church theology, but also with the ever-increasing political power the papacy tried to exert. Theological disputes became pegs on which dissenting rulers hung their independence from the papacy. The Church and state in Europe were never again to have the same interdependence, in theory or in practice, that they had during the Middle Ages.

The various groups which arose during the Reformation had somewhat divergent views of the Christian's obligations to the state. The two main movements of the period were Lutheranism and Calvinism, but perhaps in the long run the most influential groups during this period were the Anabaptists on the continent and the Quakers, who appeared slightly later in England. The thinking of these groups has permanently affected the way modern Christians view government and obedience to it. To some extent it is the Anabaptist heritage which has largely been adopted by the mainstream of American Protestantism. University of Chicago theologian Martin Marty has even written about the "Baptistification" of the church in our modern world.[11]

The Reformation was anything but peaceful. Dissent, and even violence, were the order of the day. Religious tolerance simply was not practiced. Religious dissenters were often the victims of violent and brutal deaths for their beliefs. Protestants and Catholics were very intolerant of each other, and both persecuted the Anabaptists.

**Luther.** Luther viewed the state and Christian disobedience quite differently than did his Catholic predecessors. His well-known doctrine of two kingdoms, that of God and that of the world, saw the church and the state not as part of the same Christian world, but as separate realms:

There are few true believers and still fewer who live a Christian life, who do not resist evil and indeed themselves do no evil. . . . For this reason God has ordained two governments: the spiritual, by which the Holy Spirit produces Christians and righteous people under Christ; and the temporal, which restrains the un-Christian and the wicked so that—no thanks to them—they are obliged to keep still and to maintain an outward peace.[12]

Both worlds were subject to God's law, but neither was to exert coercive power over the other. The Church, however, was clearly to have the freedom within the state to do its spiritual work. As for the state, Luther said, "first fill the world with real Christians before you attempt to rule it in a Christian and evangelical manner. . . . it is out of the question that there should be a common Christian government over the whole world, or indeed over a single country . . . for the wicked always outnumber the good." The Christian was to take part in civil affairs, not in order to Christianize secular institutions, but because they are a part of God's lawful works.

This world, its culture and institutions is indeed deeply touched by human depravity. Unlike the Thomistic synthesist who rejoices in the rationality of law and culture, Luther noted the pervasiveness of the lust for power and that in all of culture there is egotistic, godless perversion. Yet, in what Niebuhr calls a paradox fundamental to dualism, Luther argued that the kingdom of the world was established by God to restrain, stop, and punish evil and to promote positive good. Since the state bears the sword as "God's minister and the servant of his wrath," Luther emphasized that disobedience is a sin "worse than murder, unchastity, theft, dishonesty and all that goes with them," since the practice of government and the administration of justice are divine offices. Some Lutheran traditions have taken the extreme position that no matter what state exists at a particular time, it is the state that God desires to exist. In contrast, in the Kingdom of God, the Christian is obligated, in dealing with his neighbor, to bear evil without resistance, and may act with violence only upon the insistence of the state.

Such a separation of spheres leads to an abdication of public responsibility and an implied endorsement of the status quo. H.R. Niebuhr notes, "Conservativism is a logical consequence of the tendency to think of law, state and other institutions as restraining forces, dykes against sin, preventers of anarchy, rather than positive agencies."[13] Many have suggested that this thinking led to the ease with which the Lutheran church acquiesced in Hitler's rise four hundred years later.

The state's duty is to use its authority according to the divine law. If rulers refuse to be subject to such higher law, they are "tyrants" who may be deposed from office. At times, one is obliged to be civilly disobedient: "But if as often happens the temporal powers . . . would compel a subject to do something contrary to the will of God or hinder him from doing what God commands, obedience ends and the obligation ceases. In such case a man has to say what St. Peter said to the rulers of the Jews, 'We must obey God rather than men.'"[14] Such disobedience must be passive and non-resistant. "For the governing authority is not to be resisted with force, but only by confession of the truth. If it is influenced by this well and good; if not you are excused; you suffer wrong for God's sake." Alternatively, Luther advised the believers to go into exile.

Luther's own encounters with the papacy and Emperor Charles V over his "heretical" reformed views demonstrate not only his desire to challenge ecclesiastical authority, but also his willingness to disobey civil ones as well. After he was excommunicated by the Roman church as a heretic, he was declared an outlaw and turned over to the state for burning.

Because Luther was a German, Charles V, as Holy Roman Emperor, was required to hold a hearing on his case before Luther could be killed. The hearing was held before the Imperial Diet in Worms. Asked to recant his "heretical views," Luther refused to do so unless corrected on the basis of the Word of God. Although Luther refused to submit to the authority of the twenty-four noblemen-judges who were questioning him, he did not dispute their right to that authority. He declared, "I have sought nothing but the reformation of the Church according to holy scripture. I would suffer death and infamy, give up life and reputation for His Imperial Majesty and the Empire. I make no reservation except the right to confess the Word of God."

On May 26, 1521, the Edict of Worms was signed, Lutheranism was outlawed, and Luther was declared a "devil in the garb of a monk." There was no doubt, Luther was now a condemned heretic and could be killed by anyone. During Luther's journey back to Saxony, friends arranged for his abduction and kept him in hiding for about ten months. While in hiding, he continued to write pamphlets and letters criticizing the Roman Church in violation of the Edict. Later he advised those who owned and circulated outlawed literature not to turn in "a single page, not even a letter on pain of losing their salvation." However, as Luther and Lutheranism gained popularity, the Edict of Worms proved unenforceable.

Despite his own experience with religious intolerance, Luther did not prove to be the harbinger of religious liberty. Once Lutheranism was established and the German princes converted, he became less and less tolerant of the difference within Lutheran circles and totally intolerant of the Anabaptist sects springing up throughout Germany.

**Calvin.** While Luther was the catalyst of the Reformation, Calvin was its architect. It was Calvinism which largely came to dominate Protestant religious thought and practice, not only in Western Europe but also in the New World.

For John Calvin and his spiritual heirs, the faith was an all-embracing reality, affecting public life as much as private life. While human institutions may have assigned responsibilities in certain spheres, God's sovereignty reigns over all. Although he viewed the state and church as distinct institutions, they were not to be at variance with one another. Like Augustine, he saw the occasion or cause of civil government to be the fall of man, and like Luther he acknowledged the depth of sin. However, to Calvin, civil order did not have a value of its own apart from the ordinances of God. Rather, "all kings of the earth have been placed on their thrones by the hand of God and the kingdoms of this world are appointed by the decree of heaven." History is the story of God's continued creative and sovereign work, God's encounter with man.

The very idea of *society* in Calvinism is to restore a "holy community"—a Christocracy in which God is glorified in all. It was the state's function to "cherish and support the external worship of God, to preserve the pure doctrine of religion, to regulate our lives in a manner requisite to the society of men, to form our manners to civil justices." The determination of pure "religion" was left to the church. The church was not to rule the state, but had a higher calling "because it was the guardian of the Word of God from which all authority in church and state derived."

In a Calvinistic regime people should regard the local government as ordained by God. Should the government fail to do that which it was ordained by God, it might be properly resisted. However, "If anything in a public ordinance requires amendment, let them not raise a tumult or put their hands to the task—all of them ought to keep their hands bound . . . let them commit the matter to the judgment of the magistrate whose hand alone is free." In fact, Calvin advocated obedience even to tyrannical rulers: "Most people are in the habit of inquiring too closely by what right power has been attained, but we ought to be satisfied by this alone, that we see that they exercise power."

Thus, Calvin thought that the Christian's duty was to obey the state so that it could maintain the social order and preserve the true gospel. How was the state to preserve this true religion? One means was to suppress any and all dissent from the recognized, Calvinist church. Much more fanatical in this regard than Luther, Calvin became unscrupulous when the authority of his doctrine was at stake. The most famous example of his fanaticism in action was in the trial and death of Servetus.

Servetus was a Spanish physician turned theologian who had written a book, *Christianismi Restitutio,* which offended Calvin. So outraged was Calvin that upon receiving the book he wrote to a friend:

> Servetus wrote to me lately, and besides his letter he sent me a great volume full of his ravings. . . . He declares himself ready to come hither if I wish him to; but I will pledge not my faith to him; for if he did come here, I would see to it, in so far as I have authority in this city that he should not leave it alive.

In 1553, after escaping from imprisonment by Catholic authorities for his views, Servetus appeared one Sunday in Calvin's church in Geneva. On his way out of the service he was arrested. Initially Servetus' trial seemed to go well for him. Since he had been in Geneva such a short time, he had not distributed any literature or advocated any beliefs that were offensive to the Calvinists. However, Calvin himself testified at the trial and engaged Servetus in a theological discussion in which his beliefs came out, and his fate was sealed. He was sentenced to death for denying the Trinity and rejecting infant baptism. On October 27, 1553, Servetus was burned at the stake.

When a government, such as that in France, was hostile to Calvinism, Calvin's views altered somewhat. The French Calvinists, the Huguenots, were often the objects of considerable persecution by the Catholic authorities. From Geneva, Calvin and his followers set up an elaborate "church planting" effort, illegally sending ministers into the towns and countryside of France. These ministers would carry false papers and false names in order to avoid being discovered enroute to their congregations. If the minister's true identity was discovered, he would be killed. Calvin's works were also smuggled into France, despite their being outlawed by the civil authorities and denounced by the Catholic Church. Breaking the laws and disobeying the French authorities were appropriate forms of disobedience, because their purpose was a holy one.

Calvin's followers were not as strict concerning obedience. John Knox and Samuel Rutherford, Scottish theologians, advocated the right of Christians to rise up against ungodly rulers. After the Massacre of St. Bartholomew in France, Beza, Calvin's loyal disciple, declared that in godless France the sovereignty of the people themselves was a final court of appeal and that even violent revolution is permitted if all other means fail. But Beza, consistent with most Calvinist writers, insisted that these rights did not run to the individual directly but only to those with some legal standing—lower magistrates and elective bodies.

**The Anabaptists.** There were also those who did not believe that any ultimate obedience was due the government. These persons, often called "Anabaptists," were the left-wing, radical elements of the Reformation. They sought not the reformation of the church, but the restoration of the simple, perhaps primitive, Christianity characteristic of the early church.

Anabaptists saw no common ground between church and state. The church was not a political entity, but a spiritual fellowship of the regenerate. Matters of religion were to be left to individuals. The Anabaptists rejected everything they considered to be mere tradition and made the Bible their sole authority. They would take no part in civil government and rejected the Reformers' notion of a state whose legislation promoted the church. Although they rejected governmental involvement with the church, they were usually passively obedient to civil authorities.

Their conflicts with government arose first out of their

refusal to accept the state-church system which the Reformers were building.

Because of their refusal to conform to the state church, the Anabaptists were severely persecuted from 1527 to 1560 by Catholic, Lutheran, and Calvinist authorities. "Martyrdom became the anabaptist hallmark."

One of the most striking examples of the strength of the Anabaptist witness in the face of torture and death was Michael Stattler's execution. Stattler, a former monk turned Anabaptist, was a respected and zealous leader in the movement. His eloquent preaching and pastoring at clandestine meetings in and around Rottenburg, Germany, caused many in that area to convert to the fledgling movement. However, his activities were soon discovered by the authorities, and he and several others were arrested. At this time Rottenburg was in Austrian jurisdiction and Ferdinand, Austria's Catholic monarch, believed a "third baptism" (drowning) to be the best antidote to the movement.

Stattler was tried in May of 1527 by a panel of twenty-four judges. His charges stated that: "He taught and believed that infant baptisms was not promotive of salvation . . . He has commenced a new unheard of custom regarding the Lord's Supper, placing the bread and wine on a plate and eating and drinking the same. . . . He said if the Turks invaded the country, we ought not to resist them."

His sentence for these crimes? "Michael Stattler shall be committed to the executioner. The latter shall take him to the square and there first cut out his tongue and then forge him fast to a wagon and there with glowing iron tongs twice tear pieces from his body, then on the way to the site of the execution, five times more as above and then burn his body to powder as an arch-heretic."

In 1529, the Diet of Spires issued a decree ordering that "every Anabaptist and rebaptized person of either sex should be put to death by fire, sword, or some other way." This decree accelerated the extermination already in progress. In Swabia, for example, the authorities sent 400 special police to hunt down the Anabaptists and kill them. Because of their belief in nonviolence and nonresistance, many thousands gave their lives for their faith. They were often executed en masse without even attempting to defend themselves. Conrad Grebel, one of the founders of the Anabaptist movement, explained: "True Christians use neither worldly sword nor engage in war, since among them taking human life has ceased entirely, for we are no longer under the Old Covenant.... The gospel and those who accept are not to be protected with the sword, neither should they thus protect themselves."

The civil authorities were also hostile because of the Anabaptist refusal to fight in the military or to pay war taxes. The Polish Brethren in the sixteenth century recognized that as long as Christians "provide money by way of taxation, there will never be a want of soldiers."

The Peace of Westphalia in 1648 failed to bring an end to the persecution of the Anabaptist groups.

**The Quakers.** In the seventeenth century, the Quakers emerged in England as a protest against both Puritan and Anglican Protestantism.

Unlike the Anabaptists, the Quakers had no aversion to holding public office and they paid taxes to keep the peace, but they did not bear arms. But the Quaker stand against tithes to support the state church caused them great suffering. They opposed the mandatory taxes used to support national churches since medieval times, because such churches supported a professional ministry. The Quakers were also often persecuted and jailed for holding their meetings illegally, particularly after 1680, when new laws made any assemblies for worship other than Anglican illegal. Eventually, the English grew weary of oppressing them. The Quakers also began to petition Parliament, judges, and the entire population to protest the breaches of fundamental law that were committed against them. As a result, in 1689, the Toleration

Act was adopted and limited religious liberty was at last a legal reality. Even so, Quakers were still discriminated against and Roman Catholics were still bereft of their civil rights and were subject to penal laws.

The Quakers in England and in the New World demonstrated an undying commitment to their beliefs and to the ideal of religious freedom. Their tactics, while completely nonviolent, were unwavering.

# SEVEN

# Modern Religious Voices

THE PERSPECTIVES OF CHRISTIANS across the life of the church on obedience to the state have persisted to modern times. Although the denominational and theological lines often seem blurred and historical events have continued to shape the way scripture is understood, the varieties of expression are just as evident. A sample of a few such modern "witnesses" might help to illustrate how many modern thinkers draw on more than one tradition in developing their "theologies" of the state and of culture.

## *Catholic Thought*

Vatican II reformulated Catholic thought on the problem of church—state relations. The most significant clarification as Thomas A. Shannon suggests, was that it "desacralized the traditional view of secular authority."[1] The state is viewed as constitutional in authority with its purpose being to promote human dignity and the rights of the individual. The state, while not seen as the defender and promoter of religion is to direct the energies of its citizens to the common good. Where this is the case, citizens are obliged to obey it. They are also to fulfill their civil obligations by voting and by participating in government so that their opinions will encourage the civil authority to act morally. However,

Where authority oversteps its competence and oppresses people, these people should nevertheless obey to the extent that common good demands. Still it is lawful for them to defend their own rights and those of their fellow citizens against any abuse of this authority, provided that in so doing, they observe the limits imposed by natural law and the gospel.[2]

The Council did not outline what these limits were. They did, however, give qualified support to pacifism and conscientious objection to war.

Despite widespread support for revolutionary movements among priests and lay Catholics, Pope Paul VI warned Catholics against participation in revolutionary uprisings because these often produce new injustices. "A real evil should not be fought against at undue cost of greater misery." Yet one may disobey civil authority if there is damage to personal rights and harm to the common good. This view has been carried forward and perhaps even expanded by John Paul II. His support of Lech Walesa and the Polish labor movement indicates that he condones some amount of disobedience to an unjust government. During his visit to Poland in June 1983, he emphatically defended Solidarity's right to exist. He referred to the union's presence as a "question of a people's right to free association. . . . It is not a right . . . given to us by the state. The state has the obligation only to protect and guard it so that it is not violated."

Polish protest assumed a clearly religious character in December of 1983 when the government ordered all crucifixes and other religious symbols removed from public classrooms. Widespread student protests led to official closings of some schools such as the Stanislaw Staszic Agricultural Colleges where students staged a strike and sit-in to demand that the crucifixes be restored. With language strangely similar to that of American advocates of school prayer, a sign placed in a church decorated with crucifixes removed from one of the schools read, "There was no room for you, Christ, in our school."

## Liberation Theology

"It is the same God who, in the fullness of time, sends his son so that, made flesh he might come to liberate all men from *all* enslavements to which sin has subjected them—ignorance, misery, hunger and oppression, in a word, injustice, and hatred, which have their origin in human selfishness."[3]

Christ came to earth and died on the cross to set men free. In the twentieth century many theologians among poor and often oppressed people have applied this truth beyond spiritual freedom to social, economic, and political freedom. The name given to this theological perspective, which advocates freeing the masses from physical suffering to enable them to truly experience the spiritual dimension of Christianity is "liberation theology."

Gustavo Gutierrez, a South American liberation theologian and seminary professor in Lima, Peru, is perhaps the best-known proponent of the movement. His writings reveal that liberation theology involves more than the development of social conscience in Christian circles. Rather, "The scope and gravity of the process of liberation is such that to ponder its significance is really to examine the meaning of Christianity itself and the mission of the Church in the world."[4] Sin and oppression require that the church participate *militantly* in the process of liberation. Liberation theology tries to assist this process by providing an explicitly Christian framework within which to understand revolution. While, at least in theory, Gutierrez does not reduce Christ's liberation to a political liberation, he does perceive human history as a continuum of happenings in which one can discern Christ's continuing liberation at work.

Liberation theology seems to assume that both disobedience to government and violence are required. Rather than obedience to the authorities, revolution—perhaps even violence—to set men free is the call of the gospel. At least one such theologian, Jose Miguez Bonino, has attempted to explain the necessity for violence.

It should scarcely be necessary to point out that in a continent where thousands die every day as victims of various forms of violence, no neutral standpoint exists. My violence is direct or indirect, institutional or revolutionary, conscious or unconscious. But it is violence. Accordingly the discussion of the theme is not, for the Christian, a luxury or a fashionable fad. It is a test of the authenticity of one's faith. My violence is either obedience to or betrayal of Jesus Christ.[5]

At first glance, this viewpoint seems to ignore some basic moral values: the human cost of violence and revolutionary activity and regard for the enemy. However, he justifies violence on the grounds that it is the least offensive means of dealing with oppression and is less costly in terms of human life and suffering than it is to hide reactionary values under traditional labels of peace and reconciliation. The Christian community's response to just revolution is to insert itself into this process to attempt to humanize it.

Liberation theology has attempted to provide a rationale for participating in revolutionary activites involving frequent instances of disobedience to the existing civil authorities. While the church has often condoned and participated in acts of disobedience, liberation theology has incurred substantial criticism for its radical, violence-inducing tactics. This form of disobedience does not appear to give much consideration to the means by which the ends are accomplished. And the ends do not seem to include the goal of converting the oppressors, just their removal. Furthermore, there does not seem to be any criteria by which the justness of a particular cause is evaluated. By "politicizing" the kingdom, adherents of liberation theology seem to indiscriminately legitimize the revolution at hand and thus become captive to a political ideology that is foreign to Christian ideals. As Richard J. Neuhaus commented, "One's impression is that Gutierrez's vision is not that of the Church renewed but of the Church switching sides."[6]

Although the Pope has condoned and perhaps even encouraged the civil disobedience in Poland, he has been critical of the disobedience that has been associated with liberation theology. In fact, the Vatican has recently ordered that the theology be reviewed. Cardinal Joseph Ratzinger, who oversees doctrinal orthodoxy for the Vatican, views the wedding of a Christianity and Marxism as an "unholy alliance."

### Bonhoeffer

Government cannot itself produce life or values. . . . It preserves what has been created, maintaining it in the order which is assigned to it through the task which is imposed by God. . . . By the establishment of law and by the force of the sword the governing authority preserves the world for the reality of Jesus Christ. Everyone owes obedience to this governing authority for Christ's sake.

Dietrich Bonhoeffer

One Lutheran theologian of the twentieth century spoke out particularly strongly on the issue of civil disobedience. His name was Dietrich Bonhoeffer. A Lutheran pastor living in Nazi Germany, Bonhoeffer joined the underground to work for Hitler's defeat. He also opposed the Nazi regime publicly, from the pulpit, in the classroom, and by means of the printed word. He denounced Nazism as a political system that corrupted the nation and made the Fuehrer its idol and god. He called on Christians to act on conscience, a conscience formed by the gospel and a conscience ready to accept responsibility for its neighbor. He was convinced that his duty as a Christian impelled him to become involved in a plot to work for the defeat of his own country. Germany must be defeated in order that Christian civilization might survive.

Although vindicated by history, Bonhoeffer was guilty of treason in Nazi Germany. He was arrested by the Gestapo in 1943 and spent the remainder of his life, until his execution in 1945, in prisons and concentration camps.

Despite his involvement in the underground, Bonhoeffer felt very strongly that the Christian had an obligation to obey the state. The excesses of the Nazi regime caused him to rethink the traditional Lutheran position that distinguished sharply between the world of the church and that of the state. He concluded that the Christian could not simply apply the Sermon on the Mount in private and thereby escape responsibility for the discrepancies between his public and private life.

Government, on the other hand, was one of the divine mandates of God in the world and should be respected as such. However, "If a concrete . . . form of government persistently and arbitrarily violates its assigned task then the divine mandate lapses."[7] At this juncture, Bonhoeffer believed that it was not only the right but the duty of the Christian to oppose that violation. Bonhoeffer counseled that "according to Scripture, there is no right of revolution," but rather that "there is a responsibility of every individual for preserving the purity of his office and mission" in government.[8]

It was the church's responsibility to draw attention to governmental evil, calling a sin a sin and warning men against it. But "if the word of the church is, on principle, not received, then the only political responsibility which remains to her is in establishing and maintaining at least among her own members, the order of outward justice which is no longer to be found in the polis, for by doing so she serves government in her own way."[9]

Bonhoeffer concluded that the German church so entirely

failed in its task that it was right to become involved with the
secular political movement which ultimately cost him his life.
Initially, he had considered adopting a Christian pacifist
position, taking an individual stand as a matter of conscience.
Eventually, he came to believe that this position was insufficient, and thus he abandoned the ecclesiastical protection
afforded Lutheran clergy in order to take on the "hidden
witness" of the secular underground.

Abandoning ecclesiastical protection did not mean abandoning the church, however. In his writings from prison he
does not attempt to distance himself from the sins of his
church. He did not condone his participation in violence,
believing that one who took up the sword would indeed perish
by it. Rather, he felt that the time had come for Christians to be
willing to take that judgment on themselves for the sake of
others.

## Yoder

One of the most widely cited writers on the subject of the
Christian's relation to the state is John Howard Yoder, a
Mennonite theologian. Yoder's books, *The Politics of Jesus* and
*The Christian Witness to the State,* have had an impact far
beyond the peace church tradition. According to Yoder, the
church should speak to the state. However, he characterizes
the Christian's obligation to the state as one of "witness." The
reason for speaking to the state is to say that Christ is Lord
over the world. This witness is not lobbying. Rather, authentic
Christian witness to the state represents the church's clear
conviction.

Furthermore, the witness of the church must be consistent
with the church's own behavior. A church that is racially
segregated has no business speaking to the state about
integration. In addition, a church should speak only if it has
something to say. In other words, the church should only deal
with such matters that present a clear moral challenge or a
serious abuse. Yoder argues that "there should be no sense or

responsibility to cover the field with the full gamut of statements on every kind of subject that might be of any moral significance."[10]

The church and believer are to submit to the state as a part of the witness. This submission is not rooted in a theology of a divinely ordained state. Quite the contrary, the principalities and powers are now disarmed (Colossians) and a new freedom and new order given to us. But even as Christ submitted to those over whom he was Lord, so the Christian submits. It is a "revolutionary submission," freely chosen. It partakes of a new kind of power. It is obedience to the demands of Christ. It recognizes the call of suffering to the believer. By refusing to seize the levers of power and assert its own rights, it invites a new order.

Such witness does not mean that the Christian must always obey the state. Yoder recognizes that there may be times when the witness to the state will require disobedience to it. However, because of one's witness, the disobedience should be carried out in a certain fashion. "As far as the Christian is concerned, the way Jesus behaved under Pilate who was the unjust representative of a totalitarian occupying power makes it clear that even unjust rule is to be accepted and resistance to it expressed only in a Christian way."[11] By focusing on the "witness" aspect, Yoder indicates that the purpose of resistance is to communicate a wrong.

He discredits the withdrawal of cooperation with government for purposes of attaining moral purity. This form of self-purifying disobedience or protest may, however, be legitimate in terms of "witness" if it becomes a dramatic and symbolic gesture. Such refusal to obey may at times be a necessary aspect of faithfulness and witness. Yet it should not be a clever means of exercising coercive power. "Such direct action, as it is often called, is in fact, an intentional involvement in the power struggle rather than a witness to those in power."[12] The danger in this form of resistance is that those engaging in it are not so interested in speaking to those in power as they are in wielding that power themselves.

While it is improper to wield civil disobedience as a political tool, it may be right to engage in acts of civil disobedience that consist of more than mere refusal to violate conscience. Acts with a symbolic character are appropriate, because they seek to arouse public opinion and because they appeal to the moral sense in man. These symbolic activities are proper where normal means of addressing those in authority are not available. These activities will be most effective if they communicate a clear moral challenge to those to whom they are directed.

By focusing on the Christian's witness, Yoder has provided a unique challenge to those who become indignant or perhaps outraged toward the state. He challenges Christians to act as they would towards their brother or sister; in love and without self-seeking motives. Certainly an awareness of the "witness" of one's actions will cause Christians to carefully consider their options in relation to the state. The best means of protest is the means that bears the best witness, rather than the one most "effective" in achieving the change.

Yoder's writing has influenced the actions of many Christians, Mennonite and otherwise. One in particular is Peter Moll, a white Baptist South African who refused to serve in his country's armed forces. Unlike most of the conscientious objectors we have discussed thus far, Moll was not opposed to the notion of the military or to fighting in general. Rather, he decided that serving in the South African army meant perpetuating his country's apartheid policies, policies which maintain the economic and political control of the white minority.

Moll first voiced his opposition in 1977 by refusing to serve a three-month tour of duty on the Namibian border because he believed, as did many, that the war was caused by the racist policies of the South African government. He was sentenced to three months in a military prison. Later, in 1979, he was fined $60 for refusing to serve a four-day stint. In December of the same year he was sentenced to eighteen months for refusing to serve a third time. Although the sentence was eventually reduced to twelve months, Moll spent over one third of his time in solitary confinement under conditions far worse than those in "civilian prisons."

Amnesty International and the Mennonite General Conference became aware of Moll's situation and organized letter-writing campaigns on his behalf. Evidently, these met with some success. About two-thirds of the way through the first year, the South African Defense Force granted Moll conscientious objector status. Unlike conscientious objectors in the United States, those in South Africa must still spend time in prison. However, they are no longer subject to solitary confinement while in prison. Despite the hardships of prison life, Moll was sustained by the knowledge that he was "suffering for what [was] right and good, and because [he knew] that this [was] what God want[ed] him to do."

## A View from the Christian Left

The Christian "left," so called because of its liberal political views and pacifist tendencies, defies characterization along denominational lines. Heavily influenced by Anabaptist theology and the writings of people such as Yoder, this group was perhaps initially tied, if it was tied at all, to the peace churches. However, as more and more Christians from historically conservative traditions began to question racial segregation and the U.S. involvement in the Vietnam war, the ranks of those associating themselves with this group began to include Roman Catholics, Lutherans, Episcopalians, Baptists, and evangelicals.

The Sojourners community in Washington, D.C., while committing themselves to a biblical and personal faith, have become a vocal and occasionally disruptive force. They have been alternately praised as a community of disciples living out the radical gospel, or disdained as fundamentalists of the left whose views are shaped more by contemporary liberal political thought than by biblical teachings. Committed to nonviolent resistance, the Sojourners have protested the nuclear arms race, American foreign policy in South America, draft regis-tration, and the economic and racial exploitation still evident in this country and abroad. More recently, they have protested abortion. They believe that their commitment to simple living and shared resources enables them to act more freely and more radically than most Christians whose economic well-being perhaps inhibits their conscience.

The importance of civil disobedience to the social and political thought of the Sojourners is demonstrated by the emphasis given it in their magazine, *The Sojourners*.

Editor Jim Wallis' article in the April 1983 issue explains their commitment to resistance. He notes that while electoral or political options should not be rejected, the limitations of such options should be recognized. Powerful vested eco-nomic and political interests often control the system and frustrate change. Strong grassroots movements are usually required to move such entrenched systems. This is done by following "a path that is at the same time a method of social change and a way of life. That path is nonviolent resistance." The cross of Christ is the pattern for discipleship and it has significant political meaning: "The clear command of the one whom we call Lord requires that we take up the cross as the means of seeking justice and making peace in our dangerous global situation."[13]

One example of the activities and concerns of groups from the "left" was the Peace Pentecost held May 22 and 23, 1983, in Washington, D.C. Representing the Sojourners, Clergy and Laity Concerned, the Fellowship of Reconciliation and other religious peace groups, nearly 1,000 people calling for an end to the nuclear arms race assembled on the steps of the capital. After a rally on the steps, the demonstrators attempted to pray inside the Capitol rotunda. Demonstrations are forbidden inside the Capitol, and over 240 of the demonstrators were arrested. Most of them spent the night singing and praying in jail rather than putting up the bond necessary to get out.

The penalty for protesting in the Capitol is a $50 fine or five days in jail. Some of the demonstrators would have paid the fine had they been assured that it would go to human service programs. Upon discovering that it would go to the court system, they opted for jail instead. One jailed participant commented that, "Civil disobedience is an effort to get the hard of hearing to listen, to get the blind and the partially blind to see."

Another "disobedient" activity instigated by individuals from the Christian left has involved providing sanctuary to illegal refugees from El Salvador. The concept of sanctuary is an ancient one, with roots in Jewish history. While carried forward by some Christian traditions, sanctuary has not been recognized in United States law. A federal district court in Texas recently rejected the argument that the United States should recognize the concept of sanctuary and a Catholic lay worker, Ms. Stacey Merki, was convicted on three counts of transporting illegal aliens. Ms. Merki was the first person convicted in what may turn into a sizable confrontation between church-based sanctuary workers and the United States government.

How extensive is this practice? The Chicago Interreligious Task Force on Central America estimates that about 110 churches around the country are providing sanctuary to refugees. As such, they are committing a federal crime. Harboring illegal aliens carries a maximum penalty of up to five years in prison and a $2,000 fine. Transporting them carries even greater penalties. Since an entire congregation generally votes on whether to declare itself a sanctuary, all members are potentially liable as co-conspirators. Thus, declaring one's church a sanctuary is no small matter.

What motivates church members to approve an activity with potential for criminal penalties? The sisters at the Manna

House of Prayer in Concordia, Kansas, have expressed the views of many in explaining their reasons for helping the refugees. Sister Zapata queried, "I ask myself, where were the German Christians when the Nazis were wiping out the Jews? A generation from now, will they be asking where were the American Christians when the people in El Salvador and Guatemala were murdered? The thing that came to mind for me is that these are people who are being killed. It's a human cry. There's a higher law, God's law. We feel like we are following God's call."

## Christian Reconstructionists

The increasing permissiveness and immorality in government and culture; the perceived infiltration of secular humanism into the government, media and popular thought; and the apparent "unchristianization" of Western society have caused many Christians to react strongly. Among those on the "right" who have sought to articulate a theology of the state have been the Christian Reconstructionists. First espoused by Cornelius Van Til in the early 60s, advocates of a reconstructionist philosophy are represented at one end by the relatively moderate views of Francis Schaeffer and at the other by radicals such as Gary North and Francis Nigel Lee. The issues targeted as important by the reconstructionists are abortion, government interference with church ministries, and parents' rights, including the right of parents to educate their children at home.

Essentially, the Reconstructionists, building on Calvinistic-Reformed base, believe that Christianity must infiltrate every aspect of life. It must govern the "material world" as well as the "spiritual world." They believe that there is a need for a singularly Christian world view. Our current battles with humanism and immorality, they would argue, are the result of most Christians' lethargic reaction to the shift of society away from what was once a Christian moral framework. According to Francis Schaeffer's *A Christian Manifesto,* Christians have shown a pietistic, platonic, and overly spiritualized response to the world. They have often shut spirituality into a very narrow area of life. Thus, the goal of the Reconstructionists, at least generally, is to motivate the church to "reconstruct" a Christian world.

The more radical Reconstructionists believe that this can take place only with the establishment of a theocracy. They "openly declare that [their] own ends can be attained only by the Christianization of *all* existing social conditions."[14] God's laws, they believe, must be man's laws, and no government which fails to acknowledge this can expect the allegiance of "consistent" Christians. Underlying their vision is a four-pronged foundation developed by Gary North and David Chilton in their essay, "Apologetics and Strategy." These four principles are first, the absolute and unqualified sovereignty of God; second, a presuppositional apologetic (the self-sufficiency of an authoritative Bible); third, an optimistic eschatology (the possibility of progressive dominion by Christians); and fourth, biblical Law (an explicitly biblical system of law undergirding the new explicitly biblical social order.) According to the authors, these are:

four fundamental aspects of Christian belief that too often have been missing *as a unit,* from the days of the early church fathers until the 1960's. Because we are convinced that this four-part doctrinal position is now recognized by a tiny minority of Christians, its influence will again begin to spread. This new intellectual foundation has come at precisely the time when the established institutions and belief of the triumphant humanist culture are being called into question even by humanists.[15]

Combined, these four factors can make effective the "theology of confrontation" necessary to complete a "successful full-scale Christian counter-offensive . . . against the humanist civilization of our day." The radical reconstructionists are confident of their victory, claiming that Christ's victory at Calvary—evidence of God's sovereignty—guarantees the advent of their Christian state. Their battle cry is "Christ or chaos, God's law or tyranny."

At the other end of the Reconstructionist spectrum is Francis Schaeffer. Like the more radical proponents of this philosophy, Schaeffer maintains that we are at war with the humanist culture around us. However, Schaeffer clearly does not advocate a theocracy of any sort. He does not want to confuse the political and the spiritual by wrapping "Christianity in our national flag."[16] Rather, he challenges Christians not only to recognize the fact that the United States was founded on a Christian consensus, but also to act to "today... bring Judeo-Christian values into play in regard to government."

Schaeffer espouses the traditional notion that the state exercises authority delegated to it by God. It is to administer justice, restrain evil, and to protect the good in society. When it fails to do these things, "it has no proper authority. It is then a usurped authority and as such it becomes lawless and is tyranny." When proper authority is absent, the Christian not only has a right, but a duty to disobey the state.

According to Schaeffer, individual Christian response to civil government that has usurped its authority can take three forms: protest, flight, and force. The corporate church's response is by definition limited to protest and force. While many would agree that flight or protest are certainly appropriate Christian responses to state oppression, fewer would consent to force. Schaeffer recognizes the potential for overreaction to turn force into violence. However, he notes that any protest, to the extent that it is compulsion or constraint exerted on persons or the state, is tantamount to force.

Schaeffer legitimizes the use of force when all avenues of reconstruction are closed. Thus force in a defensive posture is appropriate. The Revolutionary War was such a situation as is the abortion situation now. The government must be made to feel the presence of the Christian community on this and other vital issues. If the government fails to respond, force in the form of civil disobedience is appropriate.

If there is no final place for civil disobedience, then the government has been made autonomous, and as such it has been put in the place of the Living God. . . . [and] then you are to obey it even when it tells you in its own way at that time to worship Caesar. And that point is exactly where the early Christians performed their acts of civil disobedience even when it cost them their lives.[17]

# EIGHT

# Render unto Caesar: Scripture and Obedience

OUR VIEW OF CIVIL DISOBEDIENCE emerges from a commitment to scripture as normative. It is not the acts of Christians, whether martyrs in the second century or abolitionists in the nineteenth, that are the central guiding feature for believers. We do not seek biblical teachings which, somehow, will accommodate the American experience or some heroic first-century stand. Nor can this biblical approach merely seek to find some vignette—such as Christ driving the money-changers out of the temple—on which to base our civil disobedience. Scripture must not be made to conform to our experience, but, rather, scripture must judge our history. To be biblical will require a much more comprehensive perspective than the search for supporting data to bolster a sociologically or politically based doctrine and practice.

The Bible is especially relevant for our inquiry into civil disobedience. In the main, it seems no guidebook for the magistrate on how to run government and shape the state. To be sure, there are portions of the Old Testament which have precisely such a function: establishing the nature and character of the community of Israel and the law and government which shall give it structure. But most of scripture is written for people who are not in charge, who are fleeing, who are standing before magistrates, who are slaves in Egypt or about to be hauled into Babylon. It is filled with malcontents, disturbers of the peace, and advocates of a new order. It is written for a peculiar people with a dual citizenship. It ends with the image of a people under seige by a state likened to a beast, a world deceived by the state, which is the culmination of evil power. As a minority people—culturally, morally, and politically—this people must worship and live with integrity before God, but also in the unbelieving and often hostile community as bearers of the promise, witnesses of God's judgment and grace, and possessors of a secret about the universe.

Much of the drama of scripture emerges out of confrontation between light and darkness, between powers and people. Whether it is Moses' audacious demands to Pharaoh, prophets denouncing covenant-breaking kings, political intrigue between Judah and Egypt, Jesus before Pilate, Paul challenging Agrippa, or Peter and the Sanhedrin: this is the stuff out of which a theology of culture, a jurisprudence, a theology of obedience and dissent is born. We are immersed in scripture, not in mere abstractions but in the issues of obedience, authority, and dissent.

While accepting the normative character of scripture, we do not look upon the history and experience of the church as mere footnotes or commentary. Scripture itself is a witness to the action of God's shaping the life of his people in the midst of history, usually a hostile history. Biblical teaching is rarely delivered in the form of abstract rules—it is itself encounter, tension, struggle. The testimony of the cloud of witnesses gives strong counsel to us about both the content and application of these biblical principles.

Commitment to the authority of scripture does not remove or even minimize the difficult interpretational tasks which confront the reader. Rather, it intensifies them. One must still struggle with weighing the relevance of the context of biblical teachings to the shape of the normative principles, the degree to which a biblical experience or practice is meant to be normative, what implied restrictions or conditions exist for any teaching, what the meaning was of the text as the first readers would have grasped it, and what significance to give to specific terms and words employed. Our ultimate task is not to woodenly replicate the words or acts of scripture but to identify those truths, norms, and perspectives which inform the believer today. Then our task is to live them out in today's context.

The scriptural issues are complex, old, contentious, debated, intractable. We will neither exhaust the materials, nor persuade many to alter long-cherished notions. Our goals are more modest: to introduce the reader to the biblical materials which bear on our review and suggest some of the primary questions and perspectives these materials raise.

The biblical themes relevant to the issue of civil disobedience are multiple. Doctrinal themes of creation, redemption, and eschatology have profound implications for a theology of dissent. The nature of the prophetic community, the role of law in the creation of Israel as a covenant people, and the imagery of Israel and Christ as suffering servants all speak to our issue. One might also examine the biblical understanding of power, the concepts of election and calling, the Fall. To address all of these would be beyond the scope of this volume. Here we must confine ourselves to examining those texts which most directly address the issue at hand—specifically Romans 13 and allied texts, the gospel accounts on paying taxes, certain narratives which arguably involve civil disobedience, and the general teaching on government and submission.

## Romans 13:1-7

Let every person be subject to the governing authorities. For there is no authority except from God, and those that exist have been instituted by God. Therefore he who resists the authorities resists what God has appointed, and those who resist will incur judgment. For rulers are not a terror to good conduct, but to bad. Would you have no fear of him who is in authority? Then do what is good, and you will receive his approval, for he is God's servant for your good. But if you do wrong, be afraid, for he does not bear the sword in vain; he is the servant of God to execute his wrath on the wrongdoer.

Therefore one must be subject, not only to avoid God's wrath but also for the sake of conscience. For the same reason you also pay taxes, for the authorities are ministers of God, attending to this very thing. Pay all of them their dues, taxes to whom taxes are due, revenue to whom revenue is due, respect to whom respect is due, honor to whom honor is due.

Paul of Tarsus

Oscar Cullman suggests that "few sayings in the New Testament have suffered as much misuse." One historian opined that the text is "the most important ever written for the history of political thought."[1]

Traditional commentators consistently note the sweep of Paul's admonitions. Charles Hodge's *Commentary on Romans* observes that the declaration that governing authorities are ordained by God is a "very comprehensive proposition" which teaches that the very "form of government" is determined by God's providence. For Hodge, "every person who is in point of fact clothed with authority is to be regarded as having a claim to obedience, founded on the will of God." Moule similarly spoke of individual rulers, whatever their evils, being "dignified by the institution" and that Christians persisted in obedience despite "heavy pressures."

Scholars do take special note of the circumstances surrounding the letter of Paul, noting that the issue of the Christian's relationship to Rome was urgent. Many Jews resisted obedience to Rome, citing Deuteronomy 17:15 as a biblical basis for resisting the authority of any heathen king. Jewish rebellions had broken out in a number of cities. Rebels like Eleazer declared, "We have long since made up our minds not to serve the Romans or any other man, but God alone."

Apparently many Christians felt similarly. Why else would Paul and Peter make such a strong case if there were not substantial pressures and tendencies to resistance in the name of God? In fact, Jacques Ellul has argued that Romans 13 was written precisely in reaction to an extremism which had become vigorously anti-Roman. Certain Christian concepts were potentially threatening to Rome. Christian talk about freedom might well be perceived as seditious by Rome and might also be seized by Christian zealots, anxious to escape the bondage of Roman duties. The talk of another kingdom would not set well with a magistrate, and messiahs were known for their political ambitions; Jesus' crucifixion had political overtones as "King of the Jews." Hodge argued that there was "something in the character of Christianity itself . . . to account for the repugnance of many of the early Christians to submit to their civil rulers."

That the teaching of Romans 13 is intentional, a careful and deliberate response to a particularized problem, seems to be confirmed by its repetition by Paul in Titus 3:1: "Put them in mind to be subject to principalities and powers, to obey magistrates, to be ready for every good work." The points are made again in 1 Peter 2:13-17.

Professor Charles Ryrie of Dallas Theological Seminary sums up well the general conservative sentiment about the implications of this text: "The didactic data of Scripture teaches complete civil obedience on the part of Christians and does not indicate any exceptions to this principle." Notwithstanding the apparent clarity of the text, many attempts have been made to soften, modify, or otherwise limit the scope of its requirements. Some such attempts are rooted in balancing the teaching here with that in other portions of scripture. Other approaches focus directly on Romans 13, attempting to reinterpret the text itself and provide limits or exceptions within the very language of Paul's counsel. They range from solid biblical analysis to imaginative, or specious, dodges. They are all attempts to make the teachings of Romans 13 conditional rather than absolute.

## Servants of God

Some have suggested that Paul's description of the authorities as "ministers" of God creates a condition precedent to obedience—that is, only if such authorities are in fact functioning within their authority as ministers of God is submission to them required. Emphasis is placed on the use of the Greek word *diakonoi*, variously translated as deacons, servants, or ministers, to describe the status of these secular authorities. If they are not servants of God, as ministers are supposed to be, they are not the authorities to which the text refers. Employing such an argument, John Whitehead goes so far as to suggest that Romans 13 is actually "the basic text for resistance." When civil authorities "divorce themselves from God and the Bible, they become self-styled lords . . ." and the duty of obedience ceases.

Since such governing authorities have their powers by delegation, so the argument goes, they lose their authority when they exceed the scope of their designated powers. To use the modern language of agency, when an agent (servant) goes on a "frolic and detour," the master (principal) is not liable and the agent does not act with the master's authority. He can no longer bind the principal.

## Must the State Reward Good?

Another attempt to deal with the passage focuses not on the *character* of the parties (e.g., servants of God), but on the description of the *function* of government contained in the passage. The text suggests that the function or purpose of government is to deter evil and reward good (v. 3). In 1 Timothy a similar purpose, along with that of order, is suggested: "that we may lead a quiet and peaceable life in all godliness and humility" (2:2).

Thus the purpose of the state is to create an atmosphere for faithful living and if the government instead becomes an offense to good and a support to evil, one's duty toward it ceases. Grotius, a famed scholar of the law, took this position, declaring: "The Apostle throughout refers only to power justly exercised. He does not enter into the subject of tyranny and oppression." Likewise Calvin, interpreting Romans 13, declared that while "the powers are from God," they are appointed for "legitimate and just government," and therefore, "tyrannies and unjust exercise of power, as they are full of disorder, are not an ordained government."

The problem with these perspectives is that no one would suggest that Rome, the immediate context of the admonitions, was a servant of God in any moral sense. Certainly, by the time of Paul's later letters and Peter's epistle, the hostility of Rome to the gospel was all too evident. If obedience to government is conditioned on the authorities acting as servants of God in the *content* of their orders, few governments would ever qualify. This text would be more eschatological hope than realistic counsel to believers living in the empire. Any attempt to minimize the impact of the passage by reference to the character of government will fail. If comparative analysis of the "goodness" of government is the test, then most contemporary governments would probably compare favorably to Rome.

There is no limit noted by Paul, no exception to substantially modify the sweeping claims.

This notion of limits on our duties based on the goodness of government seems largely reflective of a more modern view of the state, than any view common in the first century:

Our allegiance may be radically altered within the period of a few days if events alter our confidence, but for Paul the

State belonged. . . . to another order. . . . Governments lost
their authority and sanction when they were replaced by
others not when men suffered or attempted to make quick
work of the problem of evil . . . So long as the world endured
there would be a state, and there is no ground for believing
Paul thought it would be any better or worse, any more or
less a servant of God, than it was when he wrote.[2]

The whole notion of legitimacy of government, so popular in
the Western democratic tradition, and at the core of theologies seeking to validate political revolution and disobedience,
is an imposition on the text, not an interpretation of it.

William Stringfellow, no conservative himself, finds such an
emphasis on legitimacy quite elusive, "extremely relative,
heavily ambiguous." He cites the argument of Jonathan
Mayhew in 1750, who sought to justify the American
Revolution in the face of Romans 13 as an illustration of the
political malleability of the concept.

The duty of unlimited obedience, whether active or passive,
can be argued neither from the manner of expression here
used, nor from the general scope and design of the passage.
. . . If rulers are a terror to good works and not to the evil, if
they are not ministers for good to society. . . . if they execute
wrath upon sober, peaceable persons. . . . if this is the case, it
is plain that the apostle's argument for submission does not
reach them. . . . If those who bear the title of civil rulers do
not perform the duties of civil rulers . . . they have not the
least pretense to be honored, obeyed and rewarded according to the apostle's argument.[3]

## The Scope of the Authority

Nor is the attempt to argue that Paul here is referring not to
specific authorities, but to the *office* of a government satis-
factory. This approach affirms that the office of government is

ordained by God. Government is an order of creation, providing structure for a society and the necessary institutions of social intercourse. But, while government as a principle is "ordained," the actual officers and policies of any given government are not ordained. Thus respect for the office is mandated but not subjection to the commands of particular occupants. The occupants may be judged by the larger notion of government.

This is largely the position taken by such theologians as Karl Barth, Emil Brunner, and John Calvin. They argued that the texts do not mean particular governments are ordained, therefore, revolution and rebellion are permissible. This line of thought also influenced Zwingli, John Knox, and the justifiers of the American Revolution. Stringfellow concurs, suggesting that we are called to honor the sovereign, the office, the authority. But, to so honor the office, we may have to disobey the emperor, exposing his evil.

For John Howard Yoder, such thought is thoroughly unbiblical: "Nothing in the text of Romans 13 justified the concept of just rebellion."

If all this argument meant was that God wasn't happy sometimes with the way individuals exercised their authority, the point seems indisputable. But the claim normally goes farther and excuses subjection to authorities when they do not measure up, and we are right back to the last approach noted with all its problems.

## *Exousia — "Governing Authorities"*

Another approach focuses on the significance of the biblical term for "governing authorities" used in the text: *exousia*. A number of scholars have observed that the term used is otherwise translated as "powers." It generally refers not merely to human authorities, but to the whole cosmic realm of principalities and powers, divine and demonic, supernatural and human, personal and institutional.

Thus the world's order, its governing authorities, are seen as part of these larger principalities and powers. In God's order, these powers, both good and evil, are governed by him and even evil powers may serve his purposes. But, of all the principalities and powers, Christ is foremost (Col 1:16) and superior. In the resurrection, the evil powers are in fact disarmed (Col 2:15; see also Rom 8:37-39, Eph 1:21). Yet, though they continue in this age to exercise some dominion (Eph 6:17b), they are passing away. Christ has not abolished the powers but has broken their sovereignty, and "refused to support them in their self-glorification."

This view insists that the notion of the ordination of the authorities must be perceived not as an endorsement or an affirmation of their character. Ultimately, they are to be perceived as competitors and potential rebels to Christ's Lordship. We are subject to them, but need not see them as "good."

In a similar vein, writers such as Yoder and Stringfellow note the striking contrasts between Romans 13 and Revelation 13. It is in Revelation 13 that we see the demonic dimensions of these principalities and powers. A biblical view which does not incorporate Revelation 13 has missed the demonic in human institutions. For there the distorted state which has lost its vocation is pictured as a "predatory beast, crowned with blasphemous names, cursing the Word of God, and assaulting those who profess and trust in the sovereignty of the Word of God in this world."

Allied to this concept is the argument of Yoder that the text does not properly mean the governing authorities are "ordained" but rather "ordered." God does not institute them, but only puts them in their proper place in the stuctures of his will. He "tells them where they belong" and "lines them up with his purpose." No value or approval is attached to this ordering. However, Yoder's translation has not to this point commended itself to the majority of scholars who continue to choose the stronger English word *ordained*.

## For Romans Only?

Another basic approach focuses not so much on the language of Romans 13:1-7, as on its *context* and the way that may alter or condition its application. These contextual approaches are of several forms. One common approach is to note the socio-political background of Romans, e.g., that it is written to the church at Rome in a period when Paul did not see the empire as an intractable foe. It was necessary to assure civil authorities that the kingdom of which the believers spoke did not pose a threat to the civil order of Rome. Some even suggest that Paul's special interests in Rome and its conversion, including the emperor, colored his words. Thus the passage ought to be limited in application to the specific setting of the needs and problems of the early church and Paul's mission to Rome.

But here again, the argument seems largely unsuccessful. First, the teaching is all in terms of general principles with a striking absence or particularity of circumstances. Second, Paul did not adjust this teaching in his later writings, and it is consistent with the teaching of Peter during a period of substantial persecution of the church. The text cannot be dodged by perceiving it as merely a reflection on his personal experience. There is little reason given to expect Paul's perception of the state to be easily altered by troubled circumstances.

## Owe No Man Anything but Love

A further contextual argument focuses on the *textual* context of Romans 13, especially the verses immediately preceding and following. Ron Sider, for example, insists that Romans 13 must be seen as part of the whole imagery of the cross in chapter 12. A number of contemporary commentators in Anabaptist circles concur, urging that one must first read the text in the light of Romans 12 with its strong dissenter posture reflected in not being conformed to this world (12:2), being patient in tribulation (12:12), blessing those who persecute and not cursing them (12:14), repaying no one evil for evil (12:17), never avenging yourself (12:20), and not being overcome with evil but overcoming evil with good (12:21). Such verses give a larger frame of reference for chapter 13 and in no way posture the believer as a comfortable collaborator with Rome.

Further, such persons note that the section on the state which concludes with verse 7 is followed by: "Owe no one anything, except to love one another." For Church of the Brethren scholar Dale Brown, that text qualifies the previous verse which counsels paying Caesar what is due Caesar. Yoder similarly declares that "the claims of Caesar are to be measured by whether what he claims is due him is part of the obligation of love." This latter attempt to link verse 8 as a condition of verse 7 seems very forced and hardly warranted by the text. It contributes little to serious attempts to examine the import of Romans 13.

### Render Unto Caesar . . .

The advice of Jesus to give unto Caesar what is Caesar's and unto God what is God's, is . . . on the face of it a compromise; it is nevertheless a refusal to recognize the identity of God and the emperor.

Bertrand Russell

Romans 13 is the most extensive New Testament passage on the issue of civil obedience, but it may itself be based on another passage often cited. Jesus, confronted by those who sought to trap him about paying taxes to Caesar, replied enigmatically, "Render unto Caesar that which is Caesar's, and unto God that which is God's." But who decides what belongs to Caesar?

Paying taxes was an issue for first-century Jews, and apparently for Christians too, since Paul felt he had to counsel payment. The passages about taxes reflect a context of an urgent issue demanding a word of guidance. The implication is that there were those who believed the gospel might have called for tax resistance. It is still debated.

Tax resisters have become common. Church of the Brethren seminary professor Dale Brown says that taxes are an "issue [which] should stir the conscience of all who choose for ourselves as post-adolescents." John Stoner speaks of war tax resistance as "the most urgent stewardship issue of the 20th century" and warns against the "fanaticism with which Christians insist that Caesar must be given every cent he wants."[4]

Paying taxes is addressed in two encounters of Jesus, the one regarding the Temple tax (Mt 17:24-27) and the better-known passage (in Mk 12:13-17; Mt 22:15-22; and Lk 20:20-26) in which the Herodians and Pharisees set out to trap Jesus. As clearly as the passages seem to affirm paying taxes, creative interpretations have been no more lacking here than in regard to Romans 13. Dale Brown notes that interpretations include at least four versions, three of which offer an "out" from the duty of paying taxes. One view of the text even suggests that the passage shows Jesus was a tax resister, and infers that Jesus meant to tell Caesar he could have back his "symbol of a system of death," and that the idolatrous coin of the emperor was to be similarly avoided by his followers. J. Spencer Kennard declares, "We have every reason for believing that Jesus had encouraged non-payment of the tribute."

Some have argued that the Romans passage merely says "pay your taxes," not pay *all* your taxes; others that it says only to pay taxes "to whom they are due" and we need not pay them to those who are not worthy, to whom they are not due. Surely some kind of award for obfuscation ought to be given to those who suggested that in the temple-tax account, it was the fish and not the people who paid the taxes! "Sheer sophistry," declares Brethren scholar Vernard Eller regarding such attempts to avoid the rather plain meaning of the texts. Eller takes exception to those who find in these passages some rationale for tax resistance: "At each and every point where the

New Testament treats the issue of taxes, it counsels payment rather than disobedience." Paying taxes is nowhere related to the worthiness of the state. In Rome, taxes supported a regime that persecuted the faith, promoted pagan worship, practiced slavery, and encouraged immorality and cruelty. Yet, taxes were to be paid.

## Why Pay?

Eller suggests several bases for payment.[5] First, payment reflects a proper view of money, whereas tax resistance tends in fact to adopt the worldly view that money is all important, the measure of our lives. It is the tax resisters who have "followed the thought of the world more than that of the gospel. 'Go ahead, pay Caesar what he's so hot after.' Caesar invented it; Caesar controls it; it exists sheerly at the pleasure of Caesar. He thinks it's the most important stuff in the world; but I'm not going to let him suck me into thinking the same way." Second, one pays taxes because one is free to voluntarily submit. The command to pay taxes is based not on a premise of goodness of government. It acknowledges government as sinful and demonic, but it has been instituted by God for man in a fallen world. Secular righteousness is not a pre-condition for paying taxes. This involves a theological freedom. "That's right; you don't have to pay him anything—but you go ahead and do pay him anyway. Yes, you are free; but God asks you to use that freedom not to defy the state but to subordinate yourself to it."

Third, we pay, as the texts suggest, "so as not to cause offense." This suggests a scrupulousness about all behavior, not because the state merits or deserves it, but to be sure that there is no confusion about where judgment rests. It is the world that is being judged (Jn 9:39). The witness must not be clouded by indirection and questionableness. It is the sheer innocence of avoiding even the appearance of evil which will make the state stand naked.

## *The Rest of the Story*

The Bible makes a political statement of the reign of Christ preempting all the rulers, and all the pretenders to thrones and dominions, subjecting incumbents and revolutionaries, surpassing the doctrines and promises of the ideologies of this world.

William Stringfellow

These attempts to seek relief from the strictures of Romans 13 often seem forced and inadequate. They point to the need to consider the whole witness of scripture. As Moule noted, the Romans 13 text itself "takes for granted some balance and modification by concurrent principles." A proper balance comes not so much by seeking to convert Romans 13, but by noting the other biblical teachings which provide a fuller frame of reference and solid interpretive tools.

The difficulty in taking Romans 13 as the exclusive biblical word on the subject is illustrated by Dallas Seminary President Charles Ryrie, who insists that the passage mandates obedience without "any exceptions to this principle." Yet, Ryrie immediately notes that "when the authority requires a believer to disobey the laws of God," Acts 4:19 and 5:29 become normative. But the exception to the exceptionless rule provides an elusive escape. What are the "laws of God?"

## *Obey God Rather Than Men*

Acts 5:29 provides the counterweight to Romans 13, what Sider insisted was the early church's "working principle." "We must obey God rather than men" declared Peter, and after being charged to preach no more, the text advises us they rejoiced in being considered worthy to suffer and "did not cease teaching and preaching" (Acts 5:29, 41-42).

At the root of the passage is the unsurprising conviction

that the choice is clear for the Christian between the orders of God and those of Caesar. The application of the principle in the instance of Acts 5:29 is relatively uncontroversial. The command to preach the gospel was direct and at the very core of the good news revealed in Christ.

Throughout the New Testament, the refusal to abide by the commands of sovereigns is exclusively related to central and religious duties. It is the freedom to preach the gospel and to proclaim Jesus as Lord that is the non-negotiable demand. Though there are political implications to such announcements, they are not political in the more popular sense of the word. One will find no direct examples of New Testament civil disobedience related to the issues which often motivate contemporary resistance: political rights of democratic participation, human or civil rights, war protests, social legislation, and so on. The New Testament may not specifically forbid such political and civic concerns, but it provides no examples. The command to obey God rather than man has been claimed as justification by Thoreau, Gandhi, King, and virtually all religiously motivated civil disobedients, but that principle applies only by extension and indirection.

## Sovereignty

Acts 5:29 is built on the notion of the ultimate sovereignty of God. The central proclamation of the early believer was that Jesus is Lord. That such a proclamation might bump into claims of the State is not surprising. In fact, it has been suggested that "it was in regard to the State that the Lordship of Christ met its severest test."[6]

For believers, Jesus' Lordship was unlimited, cosmic in scope. He was Ruler of the kings of the earth (Rv 1:5), and sovereign over all human governments. Such supremacy has even occasionally made its way into political documents. An attempt was made by the Reverend James Henly Thornwell to include in the Preamble of the Constitution of the Confederacy such a declaration: "Nevertheless, we, the people of these Confederate States, distinctly acknowledge our responsibility to God, and the supremacy of his Son, Jesus Christ, as King of kings and Lord of lords; and hereby ordain that no law shall be passed by the Congress of these Confederate States inconsistent with the will of God, as revealed in the Holy Scriptures." His Lordship is cosmic and universal (see 1 Cor 15:27; Eph 1:22). "All authority in heaven and on earth has been given to me," declares the risen Lord also to our day.

The jurisdiction of this sovereignty is unlimited. As Rousas Rushdoony has properly noted, "No God or religion can have boundaries or limits to its sovereignty." The Lordship of Christ is simply an extension of the first commandment, "Thou shalt have no other gods before me." The Old Testament describes God as jealous: "I am the Lord, and there is none else. There is no God beside me." It is at the heart of the Shema (Dt 6:4-9).

Such a conviction of sovereignty creates the immediate conditions for civil resistance. It is the heart of Acts 5:29. With such an understanding, resistance is not antinomian, but is actually obedience to a higher sovereignty, a higher law. Ambrose, in 385 A.D., had declared, "What belongs to God is outside the emperor's power."

## Applied Theology

Extensive biblical accounts of resistance and disobedience to authority illustrate that Romans 13 is not the only word of scripture on the subject. If such stories were few, one might suggest that they are not normative. But the biblical material evidencing dissent and civil resistance is simply too overwhelming and too central to ignore.

One need not read long in the biblical record before encountering civil disobedience. It is at the very heart of the formative events of Israel. Daniel Daube declared that the story of Moses and the deceit of the midwives (Ex 1:8-2:10) constitutes "the oldest record in world literature of the spurning of a government decree."[7] The text tells us that the mothers "did not as the king had commanded them," and the writer of Hebrews notes that "they were not afraid of the King's edict" (Heb 11:23).

The exodus itself similarly constitutes a wholesale rejection of the authorities. *Sojourners* calls it a "national cessation," an instance of "offensive disobedience" even more radical than the passive non-cooperation of most biblical stories.[8]

## Dare to Be a Daniel

The stories in the book of Daniel, Daube suggests, are a "veritable charter of civil disobedience by a religious minority."[9] Daniel refuses to obey the King's commands and suffers the lions' den as a result. Shadrach, Meshach, and Abednego then refuse to obey an edict to worship the image and are thrown into the fiery furnace (Dan 3). They are cited as heroes of spiritual faithfulness, trusters in God, and persons who chose rightly how to balance their civic and spiritual duties.

Some liberal scholars who place the book of Daniel later in Old Testament history, even suggest the book is essentially designed to encourage passive resistance to the vile edicts of Antiochus Epiphanes IV whose persecution of the Jews has become legendary.

*Sojourners* calls Esther "a plot that . . . turns on series of acts of non-cooperation to a pagan ruler." Vashti refuses a command of King Ahasuerus, Mordecai refuses to pay homage to the governor Haman, and Esther risks a breach of the visitation rules of the King.

What of Rahab (Jos 2:4-6)? It is her deception which is at the heart of Israel's successful overthrow of Jericho. This "pious subterfuge . . . hinged upon deceit," as one commentator noted, is highly praised. Deception certainly does not seem to be "honoring" civil authority. But deception occurs on more than one occasion in scripture. Jim West insists the story of

Rahab is "not an island by itself, but one of many in a vast archipelago" of deception, citing similar stories of Jael's tricking of Sisera (Jdg 4:18-21; 5:24-27) and Jeremiah's lie to the princes (38:24-28).

Nor are such instances confined to the Old Testament. The Apostles seemed constantly to be confronted by authorities. Peter refuses to pay attention to the orders of the civil authority, and specifically raises the ultimate issue: "whether we ought to obey God or men." Peter, far from being rebuked by God for this disobedience, is rescued by the angels from the prison to which he has been consigned.

The counsel to young Timothy from Paul presumes such tensions will continue. They will be appearing before the magistrates (1 Tm 6:11-16). Jesus warns his followers in Mark 13:9 that they will be hauled before the civil authority.

So common is this tension in the gospels and epistles that Stevick observes that "such reflect a time when . . . to be a Christian at all was to be in a state of civil disobedience."[10]

# NINE

# Civil Disobedience and the Law: Loopholes and Principles

*It is of the essence of the law that it is equally applied to all alike, irrespective of personal motive. For this reason, one who contemplates civil disobedience out of moral conviction should not be surprised and must not be bitter if a criminal conviction ensues. And he must accept the fact that organized society cannot endure on any other basis.*

> Erwin Griswold
> Former United States Solicitor General
> Former Dean, Harvard Law School

Civil disobedience may be morally justified. It may even be morally required. But it is, by definition, against the law. The great philosophic debates about civil disobedience concern its *morality* not its *legality*. As Cohen notes, "It follows from the nature of civil disobedience that it cannot have a *legal* justification. . . . Deliberate disobedience to law can never receive a justification on legal grounds within that legal system." The law is what is disobeyed.

Nevertheless, once the possible morality of civil disobedience is granted, the question does arise, both as a matter of legal and political philosophy and in the application of the law and its sanctions, to what extent and in what forms has or ought the law to "accommodate," "make allowances for," or otherwise take account of civil disobedience? Should the law take note of morally motivated illegal acts and treat them differently?

Of course, in most cultures and in most societies, the kings, emperors, or chiefs were hardly interested in tolerating civil disobedience. Such activists were, and still are, in most nations, promptly dealt with in ways which require minimal legal analysis. But, within the Western democratic tradition, the notion of civil disobedience has often been surrounded by moral debates and the legal significance of this moral claim has frequently been debated.

Still, there are no legal systems among the large, modern states which systematically grant exemptions to law violations merely because they are morally motivated. A law from which one could be exempt merely because of some self-claimed "moral" reason would be no law at all. The binding character of law, and the nature of a legal system in providing predictability and mutuality of expectations, would be destroyed.

Indeed, in many circumstances, acts of civil disobedience are treated more harshly than similar acts when done merely for personal gain because of the tendency of state authorities to see such acts as a flouting of state authority, a deliberate challenge. Rather than the illegality emerging from a moral flaw, a weakness—it arises from a moral presumption, a direct challenge to the state. Daniel Berrigan, far from expecting any special treatment or cognizance by legal insitutions of his claims of conscience, saw the legal structure as incapable of such a moral response: "American courts were not set up to offer conscience . . . a forum for actions that could only be considered, in legal skills, subversive of good order."[1]

Still, the emergence of civil disobedience in America in the context of widely admitted "moral" causes, such as anti-slavery and civil rights, has created an occasional tendency of judicial "winking" at acts of civil disobedience. Some have called for more formal acceptance of civil disobedience within American jurisprudence. A significant number of legal articles appeared in the late 1960s urging the legal system to recognize, in one form or another, the political value of civil disobedience and make accommodation for it. Political commentators similarly spoke of legal justifications.

Senator Goddell urged that civil disobedience be made "an integral part of our system of government" and radical spokesman Staughton Lynd urged "total immunity" for all nonviolent, politically motivated crimes. Some legal scholars concurred. Morris Keeton suggested that it would expand our "spiritual capital" if constitutional and administrative protections were afforded "responsible civil disobedience." Lewis Coser, thinking more in terms of political stability and social change, urged special legal protections for civil disobedience in the form of "flexible systems" which allow conflict to emerge and thus "the expression and acting out of hostile feelings through conflict leads to mutual and unilateral accommodation and adjustments between component parts."

Proposals to legally "justify" civil disobedience have fallen into three general types. First, there are arguments which are based on policy considerations such as those which suggest that American jurisprudence already contemplates, by its very constitutional and procedural nature, a certain provision for civil disobedience. Second, there are those which seek to find a legal justification in some version of a "higher law," such as provisions of international law or Constitutional protections of free speech and free exercise. A third basis consists of those more technical arguments which seek to use existing legal rules as a defense—such as the claim that some essential element of criminality is missing, e.g., *mens rea* (criminal mind or intent) or the defense of necessity. In this chapter, we shall briefly explore these arguments. The defense based on the Constitutional guarantee of free exercise of religion is treated in the next chapter.

It is worth noting two preliminary points. First, it has been argued that to speak of legal justifications for civil disobedience (law-breaking) is logically inconsistent and self-contradictory. If the acts complained of do, in fact, have some privilege which the law will recognize, e.g., conscientious objection to war, then the acts are, by definition, not civilly disobedient. When, therefore, persons seek to advocate a legal justification for civil disobedience, they are more properly seeking to remove certain acts from the category *civil disobedience*.

Second, it has been suggested that the effort of those sympathetic with the civilly disobedient to provide a legal vehicle for acceptance of their acts may be self-defeating. If one of the functions of the civilly disobedient act is to apply pressure to the legal system, obtain publicity, and sharply draw the moral distinctions between the claims of the disobedient and government policy, then to make their acts exempt from legal sanction might well be self-defeating. If the "effectiveness of civil disobedience depends, in large measure, upon the drama of the conflict between law and conscience," the legalization of given acts of protest may only have the effect of forcing persons to more extreme, unsanctioned measures in order to gain the advantage of being disobedient. Illegality is what provides the publicity and the novelty.[2]

## *"Test" Cases and Sociological Law*

As we have noted, law's social role in American society has undergone a substantial change in the last century. Once perceived as an expression of a higher law and rooted in a natural immutable order, law is much more likely to be perceived today as a more temporal, even tentative, creation of man. Oliver Wendell Holmes struck the note clearly when he declared that "the law is not a brooding omnipresence in the sky."

The triumph of a sociological and positivistic view of law has profound implications for the Western legal tradition. It certainly creates the conditions in which law begins to lose its moral capacity to demand adherence.

The social phenomenon has been clear. Instead of being a "rock firm stability" as in the days before Rosa Parks remained seated in the front of the bus, law is now, as DiSalvo observed, "the stage for confrontation and change." Law has been demythologized, (and it is increasingly) perceived as a product of a social process. We now know that judges make law, and so do private litigants.

This positivist view of law does create one basis for an appeal for law to recognize the role that social protest and even civil disobedience play in serving what Archibald Cox called "the law's need for growth." If law is a product of social forces and is constantly in flux, should not the law view social forces which press to change the law in a more sympathetic light than in a day when law was perceived more as already reflecting a natural justice?

Thus, a number of authors have strongly urged the recognition of civil disobedience as a legitimate part of the legal process. It is argued that it is an aspect of the social process of law-formation generally; and that it is specifically a part of the law-forming process in our particular constitutional system.

A. Bickel, for example, cites the experiences surrounding the Fugitive Slave Acts and Prohibition as "illustrations of a process of law formation—non-legislative, non-judicial, altogether extra-legal law formation through resistance and disobedience" which was ultimately accounted by the legal order.

Law professor Harrop Freeman goes a step further and suggests that as a part of law-formation, civil disobedience emerges in the legal order when the formal law has become paralyzed:

I shall immediately state my theses: that non-violent civil disobedience was hammered out in a legal crisis, by lawyers or those who best understood legal philosophy, as a means of effectuating change within the law when law's normal processes were inadequate or were held captive by anti-legal forces; with the intent to bring about the necessary change in a democratic consensual, non-violent way, thus avoiding war and violent revolution; and that today it is offering the most vital political movement to make democracy effective. In this sense it recommends itself to legalists and moralists alike.[3]

It is contended that our judicial system encourages, perhaps even requires, law breaking as a means of discovering and testing the law. "The system can be said to offer such an incentive because jurisdictional and procedural rules of litigation tend to demand a concrete controversy, showing a definite, not suppositional clash." Thus, as a matter of procedure, the claim is that civil disobedience "is one of the best accepted legal procedures."[4]

One aspect of this claim is that civil disobedience is a means of obtaining legal standing—part of the creation of a "test case" necessary to obtain judicial review of challenged laws. Robert McKay could even suggest that "test case" is a "euphemism for civil disobedience." "Without violation of law the adversary process cannot function properly in the criminal law area."[5]

Up to a point, this argument is unassailable. Surely, the law is in flux and a product of social processes, but that does not suggest that a part of that process must be the right, prior to an actual change in the law brought about by the social process, to refuse to abide by the existing expression of the consensus.

The emergence of test cases from acts challenging the validity of laws or government action is clear. But, it is less clear that from such a principle one may obtain the larger principle that there is, therefore, a *legal right* to civil disobedience. Certainly the motivation or purpose of the test litigant and the civilly disobedient are often rather divergent:

> A test litigant goes to court to change the law; a civil disobedient goes to stay out of jail. Test litigants view success in the judiciary as the end of their strategy; civil disobedients see it as merely additional help. Test litigants seek to alter public policy through piecemeal assaults on the law; civil disobedients seek to change public policy through a wholesale assault on the law, which goes on until there has been some permanent alteration in the balance of political process. Test litigants break the law periodically, as a stimulus for the desired judicial response; civil disobedients break the law continuously, as a stimulus for politics of all sorts. The critical distinction consists in the importance to be ascribed to the judicial decision: for test litigants the expectation of a favorable ruling is not merely the strongest, but the only reason for violating the law, for civil disobedients this is just one consideration in a campaign of protest.[6]

Further, the recognition of the necessity at times to refuse to obey a law or accept a policy in order to test the law hardly creates a legal right to break the law. What is a *right* is not breaking the law, but the testing of the validity of the law by a judicial procedure. Your civil disobedience is protected only if the law is invalidly applied. You do not get one free violation.

**Discretion: Kindly Judges and Merciful Juries.** Over 1,000 faculty members of several universities signed an advertisement which appeared in the *New York Times* calling on the Justice Department to quash the indictments of Reverend William Sloane Coffin, Dr. Benjamin Spock, Michael Ferber, and others for conspiring to counsel several draft offenders. But the newspaper editorially opined that the request "confused moral rights with legal responsibilities." The account does illustrate the existence within the judicial system of considerable discretion on the part of prosecutors, judges, grand juries, and even police concerning the laws that shall be enforced.

These procedural aspects of the American legal system have been cited as providing mechanisms for the law to take note of the moral component in civil disobedience. Official discretion exists at nearly every stage of the criminal process including a law officer's decision whether to arrest, a prosecutor's decision whether to press a case, a judge's sentencing powers, and, ultimately, an executive's pardoning powers.

Professor Ronald Dworkin, writing in the context of draft resisters, notes this discretionary role of government and its potential moral exercise.

> The argument that because the government believes a man has committed a crime, it must prosecute him is much weaker than it seems. Society "cannot endure" if it tolerates all disobedience; it does not follow, however, nor is there any evidence, that it will collapse if it tolerates some.... This discretion is not license—we expect prosecutors to have good reasons for exercising it—but there are, at least prima facie, some good reasons for not prosecuting those who disobey draft laws out of conscience.[7]

The advantages of such an approach is that the use of discretion preserves a certain flexibility in the legal system. It permits the system to give some form of legitimacy to acts whose moral justification may be clear, but not in legal rules of general application. The state may "exonerate without creating an exception, to suspend the law's hand without creating a precedent, to tolerate without recognizing a right."[8]

While the advocacy of the use of official discretion in cases of morally based civil disobedience has the advantage of flexibility and further provides a means of preserving the legal rule while ignoring a particular deviation, such discretion has several inherent problems as a means for any principled response to instances of civil disobedience.

First, it clearly fails to provide any coherent, principled posture in regard to the response of the system. Not only does it clearly not go as far as some advocates in providing a legal claim of exemption for conscience-based civil disobedience, but it provides no principle at all. At best, it may, in given instances, create an election not to arrest, prosecute, or otherwise apply the full weight of the law, but there is no development of policy or law.

Second, the use of discretion, even its very name, recognizes that it is a highly individualized process. What is far more likely is that the exercise of such discretion or legitimatized rule-departures will in fact be episodic or discriminatory. Or as Robert Hall notes, "To place the burden of decision for the exercise of discretionary tolerance on men so easily subject to public pressure seems neither fair nor likely to be effective."[9] If those empowered to make such decisions are subject to political and public pressure, are they likely to be sensitive to the appeals of conscience on the part of those whose civil disobedience is often intended to change the very ethos represented by the public and political establishment?

**Jury Nullification.** One particularly controversial aspect of the discretionary elements of the system is the power of the jury. The doctrine of jury nullification holds that the jury has a constitutional *right* to render a verdict upon its own conception of what the alw *is* or perhaps even *ought* to be. An early incident was the trial of Quaker William Penn for unlawful assembly. The Recorder of London, before whom Penn was tried, told the jury that Penn was guilty, based on the evidence presented, but the jury nevertheless acquitted him. Whereupon the Recorder imposed a fine on the jurors and jailed them when they refused to pay. A higher court set the jurors free on the grounds that they had acted within their powers. In

*United States* v. *Fielding*, the Court declared "an inherent feature of the common law trial by jury accorded by the Constitution of the United States . . . comprises the power of the jury to find the defendant not guilty, even if the evidence of guilt is overwhelming or conclusive. A defendant may not be deprived of this right."

The notion of jury nullification perhaps emerged initially out of some combination of convictions of a higher law and a suspicion that the officials' power needed tempering so that the judiciary's own special interests and propensity for technicalities would not get in the way of justice. Note, for example, the charge to the jury by John Dudley, Associate Justice of the New Hampshire Supreme Court, at the end of the eighteenth century:

> You've heard what has been said by the lawyers, the rascals; but no I won't abuse 'em. 'Tis their business to make out a good case—they're paid for it. . . . But you and I gentlemen have something else to think of. They talk about law—why gentlemen, it is not law we want, but justice . . . trust me for it, common sense is a much safer guide for us. . . . A clear head and an honest heart are worth more than all the law of the lawyers.

While the jury clearly has the *power* to ignore the law, does it have the *right*? Is it an aspect of the criminal system which ought to be encouraged? The argument in the context of civil disobedience is that the jury should have the right, and be told they have the right, to consider the motives of conscientious disobedients, and thus that defendants should be allowed to plead moral justification so that the jury may weigh such a factor. William Kunstler, an attorney who has represented civil disobedients, spoke of jury nullification as a "safety valve" and Justice Learned Hand of the jury's capacity to moderate the rigor of the law "by the mollifying influence of current ethical conventions." In *United States* v. *Spock*, the Court spoke of the jury as the "conscience of the community" that "must be permitted to look at more than logic."

Should the jury be advised of their power or right? While acknowledging the power of the jury to ignore the law, jurists have been reluctant to grant them the right to do so, and most resistant to advising them of their power. In fact, Jerome Frank argued that jurors are aware of their freedom to ignore the law, and exercise it all too often, rendering verdicts which fit with their own sense of justice, regardless of the judge's instructions.[10]

Professor Paul Freund has suggested that judges be permitted to tell a jury that "they were to decide in the light of all the circumstances," and that the judge might add, after explaining the law, "that the defendants can be acquitted and the jury does not have to give reasons." But the claim of the jury's *right* to ignore the law has largely been rejected by the courts.

The talk of jury nullification is perhaps based on a myth of the jury. Joseph Bishop, Jr., suggested that anyone inclined to romanticize about the jury should consider the history of southern juries during trials for violations of civil rights. Juries are not the impartial, representative bodies that the theory of jury nullification often presumes. Thus, even if jury nullification were widely accepted, our prophetically civil disobedient defendants would not likely find mercy there.

## *Appeals to Nuremberg—The Nazi Spectre*

An appeal on behalf of Peter Herby, a Catholic pacifist and founder of the Plowshares Peace Organization, to the U.S. Supreme Court concerning a conviction for failure to pay federal taxes, contended that compelling him to pay war taxes conflicted with his free exercise of the right of freedom of religion. It also contended that international law in general, and the Nuremberg Principles in particular, constituted a legally compelling reason for his refusal to pay his taxes.[11]

The shadow of Nuremburg and Hitler has long fallen over attempts to develop a rationale and justification for civil disobedience. One civil disobedient avowed, "I do not want history to find me guilty of the crime of silence like the silence of the German Christians." [12] Daniel Berrigan, in his appeal to the court in 1977, sought to draw a parallel between the moral duty of a judge in a small German town in 1942 confronted with evidence of genocide, and the judgments in his own case. He insisted the judge was giving the "nod to murder" as much as the German judge who refused to take seriously the reports of genocide.[13]

The commitment to avoid another silence in the face of massive injustice has led to increasing appeals to the Nuremberg Principles and international law in civil disobedience cases related to war resistance, draft registration, and nuclear armaments. The claim is that the government's acts for which funds are being raised or draft registration called for are illegal under the principles of international law and under specific treaties which under Article VI of the Constitution are binding on this government.

The Herby appeal is illustrative. It asserts that under customary international law, weapons of indiscriminate destruction are prohibited, and that nuclear weapons are such instruments. Further, "War Crimes" as defined by Nuremberg Principle 6(b) and the definition of "Crimes Against Humanity" as described by Principle 6(c) of the International Law Commission provide a prima-facie case that use of nuclear weapons would be illegal under international law, and if their use is illegal, then the planning and preparation for such use is similarly illegal.

The use of principles of International Law to provide a more generalized defense of civil disobedience has been described as the "Nuremburg Rule." The Rule establishes the principle that a citizen may be obligated under international law to refuse to obey State orders which are violations of international law.

The essence of the Nuremberg Rule argument is as follows:

a) The trials at Nuremberg were conducted under an executive agreement which implemented a treaty signed by the United States; b) the principles therefore are the supreme law of the land; c) these principles have also been made the law of the United Nations; . . . e) not only were Nazi leaders sentenced, but under subsidiary tribunals thousands of ordinary participants were tried and convicted; f) if [any] action . . . is violative of Nuremberg Principles, each American citizen who is aware of this violation bears an obligation to disobey orders which further [that violation].[14]

Nancy Ellen Abrams reflects the growing sentiment among lawyer-advocates for such movements to appeal to international law. She asserts that "preparation for nuclear war, including the manufacture of tactical nuclear weapons and their delivery systems, should be recognized as a violation of the laws of war." Abrams calls for a Supreme Court decision that the Court shall "have the last word on military policy decisions that fall into areas specifically governed by international law." Such a decision, she insists, could be the *Marbury* v. *Madison* of this century.[15]

Attempts to assert such claims have not met with success. Legal standing—the right to raise the claims in court—was rejected in a case of a taxpayer refusing to pay taxes in support of the Korean War on the basis of Nuremberg, and the same court declared that the war effort did not violate Nuremberg (*Farmer* v. *Rountree*). In *United States* v. *Mitchell,* the Second Circuit reversed the conviction of a draftee who was defended on the basis of Nuremberg, on the grounds of lack of adequate counsel, but noted the case was "not a simple case."

The attempt to draw on these principles has, however, not only failed legally, but been criticized as historically and legally inadequate. Notre Dame Law Professor Charles Rice, in responding to Martin Luther King's comparison between resisting unjust laws of Germany and the American civil rights movement, contends that rather than providing any justification for civil disobedience, Hitler "is a most potent argument against civil disobedience" since he got his own start by civilly disobeying the laws of the Weimar Republic, alleging they were unjust.[16] Louis Waldman similarly suggests that it was Hitler who "followed a philosophy and practice of direct action and civil disobedience . . . and from small beginnings of violating one law after another, he built a movement which was prepared to accept and obey the laws he thought were just and defy and violate the laws he thought were unjust."[17]

A more fundamental assault on Nuremberg parallels is made by scholars such as Ernest van den Haag who contend that the trials themselves are not clearly legally justifiable. In terms of the objectivity of the judges and the fact that two of the three charges were not based on anything "resembling a preexisting law," the trials themselves seem to have been "illegal" and thus of dubious value for precedent. Thus, he concludes "I doubt that the trial constitutes a precedent in any legal system."[18]

Even if Nuremberg made law, whether that law is now American law is not clear. Even if it were, it would not justify, legally or morally, resistance to the draft in Vietnam, for example. No German soldier was ever indicted for being drafted, much less convicted. Only leaders, not followers, were indicted and the intent of the Nuremberg principles was to hold policy makers responsible.

Whatever moral principles may inhere in the language of Nuremberg, it seems clear that the legal obstacles to their direct application in American courts are insuperable at present. The inability, unwillingness, and confusion over interpretation even on the international scene are evidence that the general norms are not easily transferable into domestic politics, even were a sovereign state to choose to make such an attempt. In large measure, therefore, appeals to international law are not so much appeals for legal justification as they are generalized appeals to higher moral law. As such, they add little to the issue of the scope of specific legal recognition of civil disobedience.

## Is Civil Disobedience Protected "Speech"?

He who molds public sentiment goes deeper than he who enacts statutes or pronounces decisions. He makes statutes and decisions possible or impossible to be executed.
Lincoln, First Lincoln-Douglas Debate,
August 21, 1858, Ottawa, Illinois

The ultimate good desired is better reached by free trade in ideas—that the best test of truth is the power of the thought to get itself accepted in the competition of the market.
*Abrams* v. *United States*, 250 U.S. 616,
630 (1919) (Holmes, J. dissenting).

One of the major efforts to develop a justification for civil disobedience in the Constitution is that vigorously pressed by Harrop Freeman, professor of law at Cornell University. In a series of articles, Freeman sought to develop a jurisprudence in which civil disobedience is "within and not outside of the law." His effort is to bring civil disobedience within the ambit of legitimate political dissent and to find its protections under the First Amendment's protections of speech.

Freeman's argument for speech-based protection of civil disobedience begins with the assertion of the central role of communication, especially political communication, in the democratic political process:

Recently, under the emerging concept of the "Living Constitution," there has been a growing emphasis on reading the First Amendment positively rather than negatively, in order to guarantee the open public forum which is necessary for the preservation of democratic dialogue. . . . [The] First Amendment does not merely protect private rights but is an affirmative public obligation of the government to keep the public forum unencumbered and effective so that the sovereign people may call their government to account.[19]

Freeman contends that civil disobedience is part of this critical communication process. "Where mass communication is available to the government and 'the establishment' through controlled news releases, advertising, propaganda, and similar activities and not generally available to the protesters, civil disobedience must be recognized as the protester's form of speech." In such a context, the "poor man's forum" of the streets, including civil disobedience, must be made available for the political process. Bertrand Russell similarly described civil disobedience as a "method of propaganda" against the establishment who officially or unofficially control the press.[20]

All that remains to complete Freeman's argument is to bring civil disobedience within the protections of an expanded judicial understanding of constitutionally protected "speech." The courts have indeed insisted that "speech," in the context of the First Amendment, is not confined to words, but includes some acts. The Court, noting the communicative character of some acts, has spoken at times of "symbolic speech" (e.g. wearing arm bands) or "speech plus." For example, the Court sustained, the right of students in Des Moines, Iowa, to wear arm bands in protest of the Vietnam War (*Tinker* v. *Des Moines*). The Court said such armbands were akin to "pure speech."

An analysis of the debates regarding what types of conduct amount to protected speech and what ought to be the appropriate constitutional standard for setting the limits on such "speech," is beyond our purpose here. No clear standard has been established. As Justice Harlan said in a concurring note to *Cowgill* v. *California*, "The Court has, as yet, not established a test for determining at what point conduct becomes so intertwined with expression that it becomes necessary to weigh the State's interest in proscribing conduct against the constitutionally protected interest in freedom of expression." Cases dealing with the issue began with *Stromberg* v. *California* in 1931 (reversing a conviction for supervising the raising of a red flag at a Marxist camp). In 1943, in *West Virginia* v. *Barnette*, the Court spoke of a flag salute as a "form of utterance" and "Symbolism (as) a primitive but effective way of communicating ideas."

For Freeman's argument, acts of civil disobedience become "symbolic" speech—political dialogue. A few cases in the 60s seemed to lean toward such a viewpoint. Justice Harlan saw sit-ins as "as much a part of the 'free trade in ideas,' . . . as is verbal expression," (*Garner* v. *Louisiana*) In *Brown* v. *Louisiana* Justice Abe Fortas observed that free speech rights "are not confined to verbal expression" but "embrace appropriate types of action."

But, while the Court has shown a willingness in certain situations to protect the "plus" of "speech plus," the Vietnam draft cases reflected an unwillingness of the Court to go all the way, or even perhaps very far, in protecting political civil disobedience under the rubric of speech. As Chief Justice Earl Warren noted in a draft card burning case, "We cannot accept the view that an apparently limitless variety of conduct can be labeled 'speech' whenever the person engaging in the conduct intends thereby to express an idea." (*O'Brien* v. *United States*).

Not only have Freeman's concepts been unpersuasive to the Court, but his analysis suffers more critically. Even if *some* illegal acts may have free speech protection, this attempt to legally protect civil disobedience affords little direction in ascertaining which communicative acts ought to be protected, or what contexts are relevant, in weighing whether such acts are protected.

In one sense, therefore, Freeman's free speech argument is

too broad, proving too much. Unless Freeman is prepared to protect all communicative civil disobedience, he has not provided much counsel. In another sense, Freeman's views are too narrow in apparently limiting the protections of civil disobedience to the political communication necessary in a democratic society. This analysis suggests nothing in terms of how non-political conscientious disobedience is to be treated. What of the person who has no interest in communicating at all, who merely wants to be let alone? Certainly the "compelling interest" of society in democratic processes may be higher against the politically oriented demonstrator than the recluse, but, the passive disobedient should hardly suffer greater consequences because he does not wish to force his views on others.

In sum, Freeman assists in recognizing *an* interest which courts must weigh and have evidenced a willingness to countenance, but he has not offered the sort of compelling case for a broad-principled acceptance of civil disobedience he set out to make. The reason is that the tools of "free speech" and "political communication" are simply too limited. Free speech cannot contain the moral component essential in the civil disobedient's claim.

# TEN

# Civil Disobedience and the Free Exercise of Religion

WHEN JONAS YODER REFUSED, on religious grounds, to comply with Wisconsin regulations compelling children under sixteen years of age to attend public schools, criminal charges were brought against him. In appeals before several courts including the United States Supreme Court, Yoder insisted that the constitutional protections of free exercise of religion required his conviction be reversed and that his refusal to comply was legally protected. The Supreme Court agreed. (*Wisconsin* v. *Yoder*)

When Levi Whisner was convicted, in effect, for sending his children to an unapproved, private Christian school, he alleged that the state standards were so pervasive as to deny him and the school the rights of free exercise of religion. The Ohio Supreme Court agreed. (*Whisner* v. *Ohio*)

When Everett Sileven claimed the free exercise protections against prosecution for failing to conform to state regulations at the Faith Baptist Church private school, the Nebraska

Supreme Court disagreed and upheld Sileven's conviction. (*Ex. Rel. Faith Baptist Church*)

When Walter Barnette's daughter declined to salute the flag as required by school officials, she claimed the protection of the Free Exercise Clause. The United States Supreme Court agreed. (*West Virginia* v. *Barnette* )

When Amish employers sought relief from participating against their religious beliefs in the social security system, they insisted their rights were protected by the Free Exercise Clause. The Supreme Court disagreed. (*U.S.* v. *Lee*)

Whether claimants seek exemption from the draft from paying war taxes, from vaccination, from zoning regulations or state licenses, or whether they seek the right to use proscribed drugs or to remove their children from formal education or other acts and omissions, the claims are frequently the same: that a given government prohibition or requirement interferes with the exercise of sincerely held religious belief in violation of the First Amendment.

In case after case, the civil disobedient at trial or in appeals insists that he or she has acted out of the demands of conscience. Like Luther's "Here I stand, I could do no other," the petitioners appeal to the powerful claims of religious and spiritual faithfulness, and insist it is precisely such conduct that is protected by the free exercise of religion protections of the First Amendment.

The Free Exercise Clause of the First Amendment does provide a means whereby the law *may* accomodate or give legal protection to certain acts or omissions which, apart from this protection, would be illegal. While technically, the Free Exercise Clause does not protect civil disobedience (since that is, by definition, an act without legal protection), the effect is often to provide an exemption for certain forms of civil disobedience. Not all types of civil disobedience even approach free exercise issues. Not all civil disobedience is religiously motivated. Not all civil disobedience is chiefly seeking a personal exemption based on conscience. The protections of free exercise are of little value for those whose purpose is to compel others to act in certain ways, e.g., protests against abortion practices or nuclear weapons, but it may be relevant to acts or omissions of the individual claimant. Free exercise defenses are therefore primarily relevant in the case of conscientious refusals to comply with some state requirement, and not in cases where the goal and effort is to change the law. Where the purpose is not personal exemption, but political change, the Free Exercise Clause is rarely an appropriate remedy.

The language of the Free Exercise Clause is deceptively brief: "Congress shall make no law respecting an establishment of religion or *prohibiting the free exercise thereof.*" What precisely is it protecting? What is "exercise," or what is a "religion?"

The concept of protecting the exercise of religion represents a concern for a variety of social and personal values. The framers of the Constitution were concerned that federal action (later, in 1940, the protections were applied to the states) not interfere with religion.

Morris Clark, former constitutional law professor at the University of Minnesota, identified a number of interests embodied in the free exercise protections including "the extreme importance of the religious principle in American history," a "heritage of rugged individualism," protections of freedom of speech and expression, the protection of "idealism which serves a valuable function in society even though the idealist's conclusions may be rejected," and the "fairness to the individual" since violation of one's religion or conscience often works an "exceptional harm" and constitutes a "moral wrong in and of itself."[1] The difficulty is in translating these principles into specific decisions. Why does Yoder win and Sileven lose? Why do draft registrant objectors lose, and Native Americans who use peyote in worship services win?

## Applying the Protections

The application of the Free Exercise Clause is relatively modern in constitutional history. In an early case, *Reynolds* v. *U.S.* (1878), the Court rejected the free exercise of religion arguments of Reynolds, who had been convicted of polygamy in the Utah territory. The Court gave free exercise a rather narrow scope, insisting that essentially it protected *belief* not *action*. Reynolds was free to believe in polygamy, but not to practice it, even though there was no issue at all about the genuineness or depth of his belief. The Court said that to permit Reynolds his practices because of his beliefs "would be to make the professed doctrines of religious belief superior to the law of the land, and in effect to permit every citizen to become a law of the land." Chief Justice Morrison R. Waite declared that Congress was powerless over "mere opinion" but "free to reach actions which were in violation of social duties or subversive of good order." After *Reynolds,* it did not appear that "free exercise" had much exercise in it.

Since the 1940s, however, the Court has substantially strengthened the Free Exercise Clause protections and moved away from the strong, limiting language in *Reynolds*. In 1940, the Court reviewed the conviction of Newton Cantwell who, with his sons, was arrested in New Haven for unlicensed door-to-door religious solicitation. Cantwell and his Jehovah's Witness followers had offended their Catholic neighbors by playing records which attacked the Catholic Church as an instrument of Satan. The Supreme Court voided the conviction, and Justice Roberts declared that free exercise was more than belief: "Thus the Amendment embraces two concepts— freedom to believe and freedom to act." While Roberts went on to insist that the freedom to act was not absolute, at least it was embraceable in free exercise.

In 1963, in *Sherbert* v. *Verner,* in a far-reaching free exercise decision, the Court established the basic analytical principles in free exercise cases. The Courts now essentially review any free-exercise claim in a three-step analysis:

1. Has the government action created a burden, direct or indirect, on the free exercise of religion?

If the purpose or effect of a law is to impede the observance of one or all religions or is to discriminate invidiously between religions, that law is constitutionally invalid even though the burden may be characterized as being only indirect (*Braunfield* v. *Brown,* 1961).

2. Is there a sufficiently compelling state interest to justify this infringement on religious liberty?

The essence of all that has been said and written on the subject is that only those interests of the highest order and those not otherwise served can overbalance legitimate claims to the free exercise of religion. (*Wisconsin* v. *Yoder*) "Only the gravest abuses, endangering paramount interests." (*Sherbert,* quoting *Thomas* v. *Collins*)

3. Has the government, in achieving its legitimate compelling interests, employed the least intrusive means so as to minimally burden free exercise?

## Balancing Act

The effect of this process is to create a balancing test which weighs the religious free exercise claim against the interests or claims of the state. The test is, thus, not one that provides an answer, but a process. The test requires a weighing of claims, and gives very little clues as to how that weight is to be determined. The weighing and interpreting within those steps is by no means clear or settled. As the Court noted in *Walz* v. *Tax Commissioner,* "considerable internal inconsistency in the opinions . . . of the court derives from what, in retrospect, may have been too sweeping utterances on aspects of these clauses that seemed clear in relation to particular cases but have limited meaning as general principles."

At each stage of the analytical process, critical issues emerge. Of special relevance for our inquiry are several issues related to the first step: whether or not free exercise has been burdened. For example, what is "religion?" Or what of a general claim of "conscience?" What of claims of conscience not religiously based? These are continuing problems for which there is currently no clear guidance from the Court. If law and judicial rulings are to have some predictive element, and if citizens are by virtue of these guarantees to know the scope of their rights, then in this area the law and the Court seems largely to have failed.

## *Burdens on Religion: Definitions*

What is a "burden" on religion? Part of the problem involves answering the question: what is "religion?" In *United States* v. *Ballard,* the Supreme Court clearly affirmed the posture that the Courts could not inquire into the *truth* of any religious claim. The case involved persons who sought money through the mails. There was considerable suspicion about the bizarre notions of the religious group, but Justice Douglas noted that freedom of religion included the right to believe in things which could not be proved. The Court insisted that "The religious views espoused . . . might seem incredible, if not preposterous, to most people. But if those doctrines are subject to trial . . . then the same can be done with religious beliefs of any sect."

But while truth or reasonableness of religious beliefs is not directly subject to Court inquiry and irrelevant for free-exercise claims, the *sincerity* of the individual's beliefs may be assessed. Thus, while the Court sustained free-exercise claims in the case of long-standing beliefs of Native Americans who used peyote in religious ceremonies, they rejected a claim by a "peyote preacher" who wanted to use such drugs for alleged religious purposes. Similarly, a U.S. district court was suspicious when an alleged religious group calling themselves the "Boo-Hoos" and using a "church" motto of "Victory over Horseshit" sought federal drug regulation exemptions on free-exercise grounds.

Can the Court really assess sincerity without inexorably weighing reasonableness? Does support for religiously based exemption require of the state some theology which assists in weighing the worth of the exemption? Morris Clark says yes, insisting, that, "Unless a court is to assume the religious value of all religious practices . . . it must develop a sort of 'rudimentary natural theology' to determine which deviant religious practices should be permitted to leaven national life."[2]

Further, the Courts have continued to insist that the claimed exemption be religious, and not merely personal preference or general ethical principle. The religious belief apparently need not emerge from a traditional religious body with a belief in God.

Several factors seem increasingly to be pushing the protections of free exercise beyond more narrow images of religion. Certain of these factors are inherent in the ambiguity of the terminology itself. The notion of "religion" is, itself, often ambiguous in a pluralistic society such as America with a mix of ancient and traditional religions, a host of new varieties, and no little sprinkling of dubious claims. What shall the courts accept as religion without getting into issues of "truth" and without favoring old-time religions and penalizing new versions? The concept of "religion" must be kept broad in order to avoid an impermissible establishment of traditional religious forms or groups. In *United States* v. *Seeger* the Court tested religiosity for purposes of the conscientious objector statute as "whether a given belief that is sincere and meaningful occupies a place in the life of its possessor parallel to that filled by orthodox belief in God of one who clearly qualifies for the exemption."

## Conscience Equals Religion?

A particularly troubling area for the application of the Free Exercise Clause is the extent to which "conscience" is subsumed within the concept of religion in the First Amendment

Historically, a case can be made that some form of freedom of conscience was inherent in the Framers' concept of free exercise. Madison's original proposal for a bill of rights provision read: "The civil rights of none shall be abridged on account of religious belief or worship, nor shall any national religion be established, nor shall the full and equal rights of conscience be in any manner, or on any pretence, infringed." Later the House of Representatives adopted a version that read "Congress shall make no laws touching religion, or infringing the rights of conscience."

Contemporary commentators have urged a recognition of conscience directly. Harrop Freeman advocates First Amendment protection of conscience, urging that "we begin to protect the right of love and conscience against the State." Conscience is a mark of personal maturity, and "challenging the state in conscience may be the only way to insure that the state acts in conscience and consequently becomes mature."[3]

Clark suggests that there should be special recognition of conscience based claims. He urges the creation of a presumption that the state ought not to compel one to act against conscience:

When an individual because of a compelling conscientious belief refuses to perform any duty of positive action

established by the state, there exists a constitutional presumption that the state can satisfy its needs either by
performing the act on his behalf or by placing upon him an
alternative burden of equal weight or both. Unless it
overcomes this presumption, the state may not attempt to
coerce his will by civil contempt or punish his refusal by
criminal sanctions. . . . The state may enforce all its laws
prohibiting positive actions except that a similar presumption of privilege exists concerning those actions whose
performance an individual's conscience deems an inexcus-
able duty and which involve directly only himself and other
fully consenting persons.[4]

Such presumptions, Clark urges, "serve to maintain a measure
of judicial flexibility" which would be lost by the established
legal rules.

Childress observes that our modern liberal society is made
up of "members who are strangers because of differences
regarding fundamental values," and suggests that it is often
essential to "fall back to secondary values" and that among
these are those of "conscientiousness and sincerity."

The courts have at times spoken as if rights of conscience
were synonomous or least included in free exercise protections. Douglas, dissenting in *Gillette*, argued:

It is true that the First Amendment speaks of the free
exercise of religion, not the free exercise of conscience or
belief. Yet conscience and belief are the main ingredients of
First Amendment rights. They are the bedrock of free
speech as well as religion. The implied First Amendment
right of "conscience" is certainly as high as the "right of
association." . . . Some have indeed thought it higher.[5]

## A Burden?

The first step, besides involving questions of definition,
requires showing that the government policy "burdens" free

exercise of religion. Following *Sherbert,* which spoke of both direct and indirect burdens, and which found a burden in the denial of a benefit (unemployment compensation), it seemed that this would not prove a significant barrier. "Burdens" seem broadly conceived in *Sherbert.* Recent cases suggest, however, that this first hurdle may not be so easily passed. In *Bob Jones University,* the Court found that the government policy of denying exemption to the school was not a burden on free exercise since the school could still continue to function, but without the exemption. This seems something of a retreat from *Sherbert*'s insistence that conditioning a benefit on a decision against one's religious convictions was a burden which required the showing of a compelling interest.

## The Fox Guarding the Hen House?

Once one establishes that one's free exercise is burdened, the state must show a "compelling interest" or you win. It is usually not difficult for the state to establish some interest—for example, health, safety, public welfare, educated citizenry, economic regulation, etc. The question is whether that interest is compelling. This is precisely the point where most free-exercise claims are won or lost. It is here that serious challenges to contemporary government expectations and operative policies are likely to run amuck.

It is uncertain how great a government interest there must be to override a free-exercise claim. In *Wisconsin* v. *Yoder,* the state was required to show a "compelling interest." In *U.S.* v. *Lee,* it was an "overruling governmental interest," and an "overriding interest" in *Bob Jones University* v. *U.S.*

While no clear guidelines have been established for balancing the interests, Professor Gianella of Villanova suggested a widely cited test indicating the factors in the balance:

A thorough balancing test would measure three elements of the competing government interest: first, the importance of the secular value underlying the government regulation; second, the degree of proximity and necessity that the chosen regulatory means bears to the underlying value; and third, the impact that an exemption for religious reasons would have on the overall regulatory program. This assessment of the state's interest would then have to be balanced against the claim for religious liberty, and would require calculation of two factors: first, the sincerity and importance of the religious practice for which special protection is claimed; and second, the degree to which the government regulation interferes with that practice.[6]

But, when it comes down to it, who will decide? Government! Of course an independent judiciary is not bound to find compelling what other branches of government may. In significant cases in fact, the courts have shown themselves willing to limit state claims, such as in *Yoder* and *Sherbert*. But as a society becomes more pervasively secular, the world views of the judiciary are not likely to differ dramatically from other segments of the public. At some point, the secularist may find it difficult to understand the concept of a religious commitment. To some extent that is the problem in much of the church-state debates in education today. The secularist perceives education as neutral and secular. To many Christians, however, education is profoundly religious. A church school is, therefore, a thoroughly religious activity which ought to be no more subject to unjustified state standards than are worship services. Similarly, the State may perceive sex education as a secular subject and be totally unable to perceive how, for many Christian parents, issues of religious liberty are at stake when children are compelled to participate in the state's "neutrality."

If free exercise may be overcome by the government claiming a compelling interest, how does one avoid the problem of prevailing values in the society becoming, almost by definition, "compelling?" The more the culture accepts a given value system as normative the more they will see it as compelling. Other views are likely to be seen as idiosyncratic if not unhealthy, narrow, and constraining. This was precisely the concern in the *Bob Jones University* v. *United States* case, which pitted government "public policy" against a bonafide (even if highly objectionable, to most Christians) religious viewpoint. The widespread concern in the case was not so much the particular balancing of racial categorization versus religious freedom, as the problem of permitting a taxing body to use the principle of "public policy" to grant or deny tax exemption to religious bodies. What other "public policies" will be found compelling, and what other privileges or powers may be denied? Could a religious group with policies contrary to those of the "public" be denied permits, licenses, corporate status?

Further, as government's interests expand, and as the zone of its involvement expands, it is increasingly likely to identify those interests as compelling. One can see, for example, the degree to which government interests in education have grown from none at all at the founding of the nation, to the point where a state may successfully claim, as was done in Nebraska, that regardless of the effectiveness of a private school, there is a compelling interest in a license or other indicia of state approval. Compelling had come to mean complying. A similar thing has happened in regard to parental rights where state interests with all the state's values and conceptions, are now likely to overwhelm parental and religious claims.

The compelling interest test, of necessity, must involve weighing values, and the more out of touch a body is with contemporary culture, the less likely its values will seem significant, and the more weight will be given the state's values. The Free Exercise Clause, if vigorously preserved, may provide for a healthy pluralism and avoid the clashes of civil disobedience. A constricted free exercise protection will tragically force persons to compromise their convictions and conscience, or confront the state.

The balancing test has another, rarely noted, but evident effect. Since individuals with highly idiosyncratic views who merely want to be left alone, pose little threat to the state, courts seem quite willing to grant them free exercise claims. The most successful free-exercise litigants are the unusual, even cultic. When significant numbers seek exemption, the threat to the system is more apparent, and the free-exercise claim, perhaps, less likely to prevail. But where similar protections are sought by organizations such as religious ministries, the courts seem far more reluctant and unsympathetic.

## Conclusion

The Free Exercise Clause provides some means for creating a right of conscientious exemptions, absent a compelling state interest. Its spirit can create a safety valve for protecting genuine religious dissent. However, it certainly provides no firm and predictable basis for the exercise of religious convictions in the face of criminal and civil law. It is virtually useless in the context of civil disobedience that has a goal of political change. Prophets are not good candidates for free-exercise exemptions. The presumptions urged by Clark and Childress, if adopted by our society, would go far to protect conscience, but there is little indication they will be observed.

It is unlikely that free exercise rights will be expanded to encompass more than the individual dissenter, and even then only when state interests are small and the number of disobedients insignificant. Even in the case of the dissenter, the legal protections of free exercise will run into a public, and often even judicial, perspective which fails to appreciate why the dissenter is unwilling to accept his or her social and political duty of accepting the majority decision in our democratic tradition. Too often, the dissenter or disobedient is seen as a quirky social malefactor who may be tolerated, but, if so, reluctantly. Rarely will the society view with excitement the fact that one or more of its citizens has chosen to act in accord with conscience. And in any event, substantial state powers and interests are not likely to be reduced by free-exercise analyses. Yoder can stay home if he wishes, but the big boys on the big issues are losers!

# ELEVEN

# The Bottom Line

S O WHERE DOES ALL of this history, theology, biblical data, and experience take us? What are we to make of the calls to civil resistance? When confronted with challenges to join Nebraska pastors in a civilly disobedient protest, or to sit in at nuclear silos or abortion clinics, what shall we say?

Certainly, the bottom line is not a mere function of public opinion. The very nature of civil disobedience almost assures that such conduct, at least at the outset, will be rejected. Both as a matter of general principles and in specific instances, majorities have little sympathy for civil disobedience. It is perceived as cheating—not playing by the legal rules, "taking the law into your own hands." Most Christians today view civil disobedience as unnecessary, immoral, unbiblical. But majorities cheered lions, not Christians; Hitler, not Bonhoeffer. We shall have to go beyond polls and surveys.

Further, we acknowledge the urgency of the issues which increasingly face the morally sensitive citizen and believer. Whether one looks chiefly at government intrusion into the religious sphere, the socio-moral issues of abortion and pornography, the issues of nuclear war and peace, or the classic arenas of civil and human rights, the questions are not ones of mere personal inconvenience. They go to the core issues of morality, justice, and righteousness. They are inescapably urgent and insistent. Nor do the postures of these issues seem amenable to easy compromise or neutrality. Neutrality in the face of the enormity of evil before us is incomprehensible. Neutrality or compromise about the integrity of human life, abortion, human rights around the world, or nuclear catastrophe seems as absurd as it is illogical.

What follows, then, is an attempt to identify some basic principles which we believe are biblically sound and consistent and which point out relevant factors for the individual and the church faced with such issues and decisions. We have sought, up to this point, to present a broad range of opinion and introduce the complexity of the issue in the hope that it would assist you in evaluating this area of discipleship. Probably, we have loaded the deck somewhat and our biases have doubtless crept in. At times, we have deliberately suggested important perspectives. Here, we will be more direct, but, we hope, not directive.

*Canon: One's basic presuppositions and theologies, both in general and especially in regard to the relationship of the Christian to the state and culture, will have a profound impact on the way in which civil disobedience is viewed both in the abstract and in given contexts.*

Deeply shaping any view of civil disobedience, its legitimacy, and its proper occasions will be one's theology of the state or theology of culture. What one believes about the role of government, the place of the state in God's order, the relationship of the Christian to society and state is highly critical for any analysis of civil disobedience. It shapes not only one's decisions about what state actions are appropriate, but what one may expect from the state and the degree to which one ought to seek to shape the policies of the state and the character of contemporary culture.

The answers to these questions by an Anabaptist or a modern Tertullian, in the tradition of opposition to culture and the state as instruments of principalities hostile to God's new order, would be quite different from one who sees this order as one in which God is moving to establish his Lordship, as, for example, a Calvinist.

The effect of one's theology is even seen in areas apart from formal views of the state. One's doctrine of eschatology, for example, may well shape one's response to civil evil. (Eschatology refers to our doctrines of the last things, the end times.) What is it we shall look for? How will God's purposes be manifested? If an emphasis is on the return of Christ in the midst of a decaying world—a premillenial view—then this age is seen to be passing away. If a new one is about to be brought in by the imminent return of Christ, and a new order built on the ashes of this world, then one may be much more likely to merely seek survival. Such persons will have little interest in the structures of this world, in seeking to shape the arts and sciences with the new age about to dawn. They are more likely to want to be left alone. They emphasize doctrines of redemption, salvation, and conversion. The state and law, it is hoped, will restrain evil as much as possible and allow room for the gospel, but even this is ultimately hopeless. It is best not to be caught up in the entanglements of this world. It is best to focus upon your citizenship in heaven and not in this world, in which you are strangers and pilgrims.

Alternatively, if one's eschatology, as in a postmillenial view, perceives God's people acting faithfully in response to God's sovereignty establishing his reign in his creation, then the degree to which one intersects with and seeks to shape the state will be quite different. Christian Reconstructionists have, for example, quite properly noted the relevance of eschatology in the contemporary American religious debate about civil disobedience. They blame fundamentalist and Baptist eschatology for the failure of such groups to claim God's sovereignty in the public realm. Such persons emphasize God's sovereignty, and the doctrine of creation. Similarly, liberation theologians and less radical social action groups reject the postponement of the witness to public justice. Our task is to incarnate the gospel in the confidence that the gates of hell shall not prevail.

Thus, fundamental doctrinal presuppositions of the sort well documented by H. Richard Niebuhr and others provide the base line, the basic world-view and kingdom-view, which will largely shape one's thought about civil disobedience. These ideas provide a lens through which civil disobedience will be viewed, either clarifying or distorting history and scripture.

*Canon: One's judgment about values and their hierarchy is perhaps the most controlling element of one's views about the appropriateness of civil disobedience, and is inescapable in the moral assessment of it.*

It is essential to recognize the often indistinct aspect of one's moral judgment which underlies issues of civil disobedience. Whether or not a given act of civil disobedience is justified will largely depend on one's values, morals, or ethics. While questions of style and process (e.g., nonviolence, exhaustion of remedies) are relevant, they tend to shade into the background of the more fundamental questions of the moral character of the goal or objective pursued, and, more specifically, the enormity of the evil resisted.

If, for example, one views a given goal, like ending abortion, as a moral value of the highest order (preventing murder on a massive scale), then the acts which are legitimate to save lives are many. Fewer acts to achieve that goal will be perceived as improper. Destroying property, violating trespass laws, inconveniencing traffic, and jamming up bureaucracies are likely to be perceived as minuscule compared to the evil fought.

To use a historic example, acts to stop the Holocaust would be defended that would never be held as proper for resisting government regulation of church day-care centers. Similarly, the morality of acts to halt an Idi Amin are going to be different from the kinds of defensible acts to prevent the election of a Carter or a Reagan. Why? Not because of secondary factors of sincerity, or process-factors of exhaustion of remedies, or methodological elements of nonviolence. Rather, the moral enormity of the evil opposed is the basis for resisting the state.

If this sounds suspiciously like a species of "ends-justify-means" morality, it is nevertheless inescapable. Valueless situation ethics rooted in hedonism and privatistic morality is always properly condemned. Situation ethicists, who see all standards as relative and who reduce moral decision-making to a last-minute calculus of what is "loving," offer only a nebulous ethical standard. The *situation* does not change the moral rules nor shift the ethical guidelines nor rewrite the Ten Commandments, but it does often provide the context for decisions between rules and principles. The German citizen asked by the SS if he knows the location of any Jews must indeed weigh the principle of truth-telling against other moral principles. The context and our moral assessment of the factors is critical.

These moral and value questions are inescapable! They cannot, nor ought they, be avoided. The issues of civil disobedience are, in fact, issues of fundamental moral values. The moral claim of obedience to law is secondary to the question of what is the higher law, higher claim?

*Canon: Saying* NO *to government is under proper circumstances not only a permitted but a necessary response of morally mature and biblically faithful Christians.*

We believe that the capacity to say no and the will to do it are not only within the permissive will of God, but at times may be biblically mandated. To refuse to tolerate, abide by, cooperate in, stand idly by in the face of some decrees, acts, and policies of government is, we believe, fundamental to our understanding of God's claims on our life. It is part of our integrity, our witness, and our declaration of the Lordship of Christ. It is, as many have suggested, an issue of sovereignty. We cannot give our hearts and minds to Christ, but unreservedly give our voices, and bodies, and wills to Caesar. It is our conviction that such a perspective is taught in scripture, is the teaching of most theological Christian traditions, and has been the witness of the church and its faithful. Martyrs, prophets, and many more untitled moral heroes have not shirked from the social, political, economic, and even physical consequences of a firm and resolute NO to Caesar.

This NO emerges from our understanding of God's ultimate claims, but also from a conviction that we are moral agents and that our moral living and moral witness is an essential aspect of our integrity and our public service. Saying NO is a capacity of morally mature persons. Underlying this is also a conviction that whatever the specific meaning of controverted passages such as Romans 13, they do not suggest that all acts of government are either approved or endorsed by God, nor that there is an unconditional duty to obey. We are not called by scripture to suspend moral judgment or surrender our wills. Thoreau was surely right in part when he suggested that there was something puzzling in the fact that we each have been given a conscience, if in fact we are not to exercise it.

We believe government is an institution within God's order for creation, and that it serves both preservative and educative functions. God wills and orders it to do justice, reward good, and restrain evil. But government is capable of massive evil. It is clearly, at times, a principality and power which is hostile to the gospel, and has no ultimate claim upon us. It can be the beast of Revelation.

In fact, some policies of law and government cry out for civil resistance; they plead for someone to say a defiant *no* to government's usurpations and immorality. Certain instances require that we courageously risk declaring that "The Emperor has no clothes"—thereby dispelling our illusions, captivity, and timidity.

Our tendency to offer some sort of blind obeisance and to grant credibility to the proclamations and acts of government approaches some mystical notion of an immaculate conception of government. In fact, government actions partake of the same evil that appears in personal sin. Governments as much as persons fall short of the glory of God. In the Old Testament, governments (nations) are called to account for their acts and omissions. "America: Right or Wrong" reflects a tragic misreading of biblical principles, however admirable the patriotism. We believe one may be justly proud, for example, of certain aspects of the American political experience, especially the growing commitments to political and economic liberties. One may even choose to declare one's nation the best, or freest, or even the hope of the world. But, one may not, as a Christian, baptize a nation's policies, acts, and laws as God's, nor add God's sanction to them.

We are further convinced that one of the tasks of the church is to instill people with a morally alert conscience, a conscience not intimidated psychologically, spiritually, or culturally into blind acquiescence. Not being conformed to the world, overcoming fear, and being willing to lose one's security are central to the freedom of which the gospel speaks. We believe it is time for the church to recognize its mission of equipping its people with informed and active consciences. Developing capacities for moral judgment and the will to act faithfully in obedience to moral truth is an urgent need. We need communities of faith which nurture and sustain persons.

*Canon: Not every act of government which is sincerely and conscientiously believed contrary to God's will warrants civil disobedience.*

A commitment to the sovereignty of God and the ultimate claim of Christ on our life opens the door to civil disobedience as a consequence of our obedience to God and a means of bearing witness to his claims. That, however, does not mean that civil disobedience somehow becomes a normative process for Christian participation in the public order. As Abe Fortas recognized, those who would reject the law have a "frightful burden." Not every inconvenience which may come to the church or individual believer or every policy of government which may fall short of the ideals or wishes of a citizen or the Christian community suddenly warrants such disobedience.

A variety of difficult issues remain for the believer even after acknowledging that certain circumstances may give rise to the duty or right of holy disobedience.

Two basic types of questions are recurring and urgent. The first type deal with how one shall assess what kinds of claims of government warrant resistance by civil disobedience. Or, put differently, there are issues of the content or nature of laws which trigger a legitimate civilly disobedient response; what, substantively, will give rise to civil disobedience as a moral response?

The second type focus not on the nature of the rights and claims, but on the process or type and style of civil disobedience which is appropriate for the believer, both generally and in a specific context. What means are appropriate? What limits on civil disobedience are placed on Christians?

In any social and political structure, even as Thoreau in his radicalism noted, there is a certain friction built into the machinery. Thoreau said, "Let it go." In a highly pluralistic society governed in a democratic tradition, many policies and approaches of government will seem, and perhaps are, morally inadequate. Not every instance of such failure of government or usurpation of authority by the state warrants appeals to Gandhi and citations of the tragedies of silence in the Holocaust. There is an inevitable immorality and ambiguity about our common and shared existence. Our cultures as well as our laws embody not only our visions, but also our painful histories.

Even where there might be a clear sense of unjust law, the prudent may decline to resist. This prudence need not be seen as cowardice, nor insensitivity to evil. It may, as well, be a recognition of other elements which must also be weighed. Aquinas distinguished between laws against the divine good and those against the common good. As to the latter he counseled that, even where a right to disobey might exist, concerns for avoiding "scandal" or "disturbance" warrant a waiver of that right.

There is a level of endurance incumbent on all citizens. There is no biblical expectation that government will embody all the high principles of the gospel. It may be that the assumption is quite the contrary. The capital of moral rebellion must be carefully preserved and spent only in those places where the leverage is most productive.

Further, there is a danger today of the ultimatization of all social and political opinion. Every urgent social issue becomes a test, a focus of divine truth, a watershed of justice. The room to maneuver, to listen, to compromise is vitiated by the hardness of convictions. Certainly many issues today do in fact raise ultimate questions, witness for example the debates regarding abortion and nuclear war. But one must be careful about easily assuming that our contemporary liberal or conservative agendas are identical with God's will, thus permitting us to set aside compromise, humility, and the tentativeness of political opinion. Liberals, for example, classically condemned the ease with which many conservatives identified American values and Western political and economic life with God's will. Yet, they have quite easily made a similar identification of their own persuasions regarding nuclear freezes, Central American politics, and other issues. Right wing religious groups have similarly viewed political issues about the Panama Canal Treaty and capital punishment as if they were ultimate moral issues.

Further, it is critical to recognize that the means of protest and social change are multiple. Particularly in American society with strong and ever-growing commitments to free speech and political dissent, the avenues for political dialogue and public debate are many. The ways one may say "no" to government are not limited to civil resistance. There is a vigorous public forum, an active press, strong dissenting views in media. Such processes, it seems to us, make the use of civil disobedience for "witness" and consciousness-raising somewhat less defensible.

We believe that the combination of available alternatives and a basic respect for law combine to create a duty to exhaust alternative remedies before resorting to civil disobedience, especially where the civil disobedience takes on a public and political character. Where there are means of social and moral suasion within the law, it seems that our social covenant at least requires us to utilize those first.

While obedience to law is not an ultimate value, it is *a* value. It is easy to point to the vagaries of law, its illusions, and even codified evil. In Faust, Mephisto, replying to the student's declaration that he could not bring himself to like Jurisprudence, replied: "I do not blame you there, for I know only too well what kind of science it has come to be. All rights and laws are transmitted like an eternal disease from generation to generation. . . . Reason becomes a sham . . . There is no longer an inquiry after the law which is born with us."

But the law is also, as Holmes noted, the "moral deposit" of our civilization. The struggle to establish an order of law and not of men has been a costly enterprise. We dishonor that heritage if we dismiss law as Tennyson did in describing it as a "codeless myriad of precedent." We create precedents for lawlessness at great risk.

There is a duty to obey the law, even a moral duty. The law is prima- facie entitled to respect. It is the product of our history and our community. That duty may, of course, be overcome, but *overcome* it must be, and by more than mere whim. Something like clear and convincing evidence is essential. We dare not lightly countenance the exercise of individual authority against that of the social structure. Order and peace and structured change is an important component of the social order and not inconsequential for the development of other structures, including the spread of the gospel.

The law is usually also an expression of the sense of the

majority. Though the mere claim of a democratic majority is not dispositive of moral issues (since majorities may also be insensitive and immoral, and, when so, most dangerous because of the supposed value of majority opinion), nevertheless, we should not cavalierly ignore the sense of our communities.

*Canon: As a general rule, the most morally defensible and biblically consistent form of civil disobedience is conscientious non-cooperation.*

The historic pattern of religiously based civil disobedience was the conscientious refusal to obey or cooperate with government's demands when they conflict with a prevailing moral commitment. More recently, persons with clear Christian commitments have participated in more expansive forms of civil disobedience, including indirect disobedience and the use of disobedience not to maintain personal integrity but to further social and political ends.

We believe that direct, individual, conscientious non-cooperation is more consistent with certain basic Christian commitments, and more morally defensible from a public and political perspective. By its nature, it is almost invariably nonviolent; its moral character is more transparent; it rarely threatens the essential order and social fabric including a respect for the basic legal order; it is less tempted to pretentiousness; it does not seek to impose its will on others; it shows a maximum respect for the rights of others.

Certain biblical teachings in regard to submission to authorities and non-resistance to evil seem consistent with such a form of holy disobedience. It is also consistent with the view of King and Gandhi that the goal is not victory over enemies but their conversion.

Confining direct civil disobedience to those laws actually believed to be morally objectionable also preserves more transparently the moral integrity of the disobedience itself. Direct, conscientious disobedience of a non-political character is least likely to create confusion in the state or the public as to the conscientious and moral basis of the acts. Such direct holy disobedience may be either active or passive depending on the very form of laws. Often, it is difficult to draw sharp lines between active and passive. Was Everett Sileven in Nebraska engaging in passive disobedience by refusing to register his school, or in active disobedience by his continued operation of the Christian school contrary to a court order?

We believe that when civil disobedience moves beyond these parameters serious reservations emerge. When the mode is indirect or when the purpose becomes tactical, rather than personal faithfulness, a new set of moral issues are raised and the burden of justification is substantially greater.

Mere conscientious non-cooperation or disobedience may amount to an isolationist, individualistic response which is insensitive to the scope of evil and one's public responsibility. But, individual non-cooperation is not without its witness to the state, nor without political significance. We also encourage multiple forms of witness to the state and the full use of the panoply of constitutional liberties available to morally challenge the society. Nor do we draw an absolute line against all indirect or politically motivated civil disobedience. We do have a responsibility for more than personal integrity. Justice, for the Christian, is not complete when one secures one's own exemption from the injustice in the world. In certain situations, indirect disobedience may be required by the nature of the policy or law opposed. In addition, indirect disobedience may serve a substantial moral purpose in initially calling attention to a targeted evil, a consciousness-raising witness. There are still limits on the use of the method—limits of form and duration. Once you get the attention and make the point, the witness has been made.

To be sure, there may be outrages so great that even after one makes one's witness and society disregards it, one must continue to speak and act in dramatic ways. Mere non-cooperation with the Holocaust or a few sit-ins at Goebbels' office followed by passive resignation would have been morally inadequate. But relatively few issues possess the character of the Holocaust context: the depth of evil confronted, the total irrelevance of patient acceptance of the slowness of social and political change, and the direct policy of government in implementing of the evil. Most issues are more complex, less straightforward.

In addition to the problems of the indirect character of some civil disobedience, the political-social purpose of some civil disobedience has troubling aspects in spite of our affirmation of the role of such in the securing of civil liberties in American history. We are concerned both theologically and politically with the expanding use of civil disobedience as a political tool. Such approaches often quickly deteriorate into political power-struggles. The rhetoric is religious, but the arena is one of traditional political debate. Civil disobedience is used as a political weapon and justified as conscientiously based. The means become totally subservient to the goals.

We perceive that, in such a process, the moral component becomes highly diffused and subjective, if not lost. The moral dimensions are likely to be quickly lost in the disobedient's attempts to find new dramatic forms of "witness," new ploys to attract the media. Or alternatively, if the processes are intended to jam the machinery of government so as to compel accomodation to the interests of the protesters, the moral elements surely have been sold for political leverage. The tendency of such politically focused disobedience to involve mass action further exacerbates the problems of maintaining the moral base of the conduct, a problem King and Gandhi both faced.

Further, politically oriented civil disobedience often reflects a questionable apocalyptic view of our condition and appropriate remedies. One author speaks of our present "global Jonestown." Dissenters are postured as moral heroes, near messianic in character. The language is that of war—the opponents are evil, the state is "them." The image is dualistic.

This is true on both the left and right—on the part of Sojourners and the Christian Reconstructionists. Winning is the key.

Civil disobedience in such a mode becomes too easily a refuge for not only the high-minded, but the neurotic as well. For some, today's struggle will soon become too conventional to feed their psychic need. The events become self-justifying. The crusade itself is their source of meaning, and its purposes largely subservient to its processes. It is a religious high, a glorious tantrum.

Such movements tend not only to be self-authenticating, but accelerating. One needs more and more to show one's commitment, to call more strenuously for a new order. Violence soon becomes justified or excused as an inevitable result of confronting evil. The movement easily becomes not civil disobedience for a limited goal, but revolutionary—the launching of a new order. Mary Lou Kownaki, Benedictine founder of Pax Center, reflects this search for more drama, for a new agenda:

> Yes, we need more than symbolic action. We need the peace curriculums, the petitions, the lobbying, the political analysis, the religious statements on peace, the books and articles on nuclear disarmament. But we are desperate for something more. I think we all begin by trying to put new wine into old wineskins; my hope is that we don't stop when the wine begins to seep through the cracks, the tears.[1]

Finally, we are also concerned at the tendency to see civil disobedience as a short-cut to political processes, moral education, and spiritual formation. While the "voice of the people" is not ultimately sovereign, one must ponder how a democratic society can engage in genuine rational and moral discourse when present minorities, having failed in their political and moral suasion, now choose another level of discourse. Even if successful through the use of the leverage of inconvenience or intimidation, each success merely begs the next comer-with-a-vision to adopt the same approach, with each one raising the stakes.

For these reasons, we believe that when the moral claims require a refusal to abide by the demands of the state, the primary mode should be one of conscientious non-cooperation; the participation in the more radical forms of direct action and political strategizing through civil disobedience is justified only after overcoming a weighty presumption against its spiritual and moral legitimacy. Only the highest of causes warrants the risks to spiritual integrity and democratic values inherent in indirect and politically inspired civil disobedience.

*Canon: The biblical call to submission to authority represents not only a limitation on the character and form of permissible civil disobedience for the believer, but evidences a conviction of a new order of reality which extends beyond the structures of power.*

The biblical witness to submission to authority is well-documented. There is little question that some interpretations of these teachings have failed to listen to the whole counsel of scripture and have, thus, become refuges for conservative political philosophy or, worse, apologies for destructive authoritarianism in family as well as moral life. Biblical submission never meant uncritical obedience, the suspension of moral judgment, the abdication of the mind and will. The state is never given the power to define the scope of discipleship or to draw the parameters of obedience. Our submission is not the same as obedience. It is an acknowledgment of the authority of the state or community under which we live, an admission that that authority is part of God's ordering of our public life.

Notwithstanding the liberationists of our own day, the new order which broke in upon us in Jesus was not a political revolution. Under an often oppressive regime, the counsel to submit was given and repeated. The disciples were not a zealot team, and the temptation to engage in that sort of power struggle for the kingdoms of this world was profoundly rejected in the desert where Satan tempted the Lord.

Our submission, even when we must disobey, does surely serve some conservative purposes: it negates an unabashed alliance with the contemporary political power struggles of a revolutionary nature; it respects the role of government and the importance of a legal order; and it recognizes the role of authority in any community and society. But, it is both more and less than an ally of conservative political and social thought. There is simply too much biblical witness about the disarming of principalities and powers, about the liberating news of the gospel which shatters the pretensions of earthly powers, about the passing away of the old and the breaking in of the new, to see the Christian faith as ideological bedrock for traditionalists. Troeltsch was right when he argued that hidden in its quiet and peaceful mode, at its core, Christianity is revolutionary.

Rather than an endorsement of the status quo, a conservative political philosophy, or a pragmatic accommodation to seek to gain Rome's acquiescence, this biblical word represents something even more radical. We believe Yoder is largely right in suggesting that the counsel to submission is not based on any ultimate authority of the state. The state, relative to the Lordship of Christ and the reordering of creation, is an interim reality, at times even a principality and power destined to destruction and already led captive in the resurrection (Col 2:15).

The admonition to submit is part of a larger biblical witness about how evil is overcome and how the kingdom will arise. It witnesses to a whole new way in which truth and justice break into our world. And this new way has as much to do with *means* as it has with *ends*. The cross is not one of many routes. The new way is that of seeds that grow slowly, but first fall into the ground and die. It is a way of people losing their lives before they find them. It is a way filled with death . . . and then resurrection. Means and ends are forever linked. Our witness to the world, even our saying no must bear within itself the mystery of the cross. That is part of what submission, suffering, and releasing our rights means.

## Jesus and the Cross

Ye have heard it said of old . . . , but I say unto you. . . .
Jesus of Nazareth

The central motif of such principles is the model of Christ, who, though Lord of all, did not grasp after his prerogatives, but humbled himself even unto death (Phil. 2:6-8). The acceptance of injustice, and the suffering and servanthood of Christ and the church are not intended to silence the witness of the faithful, but to base that witness on a new and different kind of power. There is in this a rejection of the political calculus and the suggestion of a whole new creation which is being born. Martin Buber, the Jewish theologian, noted how "contrary to history" and "against nature" is the whole biblical notion of what really "is" and what constitutes power.

It emerges out of a conviction that the real orders of this world will not be changed by more effectively structured civil disobedience—and more dramatic witness. It will not be the mail lists, political campaigns, the picketing, or the jail sentences that shatter this worldly order. Rather it is suffering servants, crucified Lords, remnant nations, slain lambs, earthen vessels that bear in their lives the covenant. The sign of power is not the scepter, but the cross: "Worthy is the lamb that was *slain* for he shall receive power" (Rev 5:12).

This conviction that the last shall be first and that the weak things will confound the mighty seems an escape to many a political activist. It smacks of religion as an opiate, an irrelevance, a pie in the sky kind of illusion. And, of course, it can be. That is not, however, its biblical intent. It is true that it is not a political strategy; it is not a clever underdog tactic. It is a principle, a reflection of the divine order, not a ruse. It is not an ethic for the interim. It is a reflection of a new order. It hears clearly the word of God that the victory is not by might nor by power, but by his spirit. John Howard Yoder puts it bluntly, "suffering and not brute power determines the course of history."

Neither silence, nor flight, it is a new way of speaking and a new way of being present. Not powerful or successful, it is a way that appears helpless, tragic. Herbert Schlossberg has expressed well the combination of faith in the Lord of history with the recognition that our ability to grasp it is grounded in futility:

> We do not pretend that the fate of the world is in our hands. That way lies madness, being a burden that no human being can bear. Yet we are not condemned to resignation and quietism, still less to despair. We are not the lords of history, and do not control its outcome, but we have assurance there is a Lord of history and he controls its outcome. We need a theological interpretation of disaster, one that recognizes that God acts in such events as captivities, defeats, crucifixions. The Bible can be interpreted as a string of God's triumphs disguised as disasters.[2]

Our capacity to insert a new dynamic, to get leverage on the world by standing within a new reality, may indeed depend on our will to engage the world a new way. In biblical history, the way to gain leverage in history is to challenge directly its presumptions of power by powerlessness, to refuse to trust in chariots and alliances. David Burrell and Stanley Hauerwas have strikingly linked suffering to our capacity for public responsibility:

> The complicity of Christians with Auschwitz did not begin with their failure to object to the first slightly anti-semitic

laws and actions. It rather began when Christians assumed they could be the heirs and carriers of the symbols of the faith without sacrifice and suffering. . . . Persons had come to call themselves Christians and yet live as though they could avoid suffering and death. So Christians allowed their language to idle without turning the engines of the soul . . . their lives were seized by powers that they no longer had the ability to know, much less to combat.[3]

It is really the person who can see the world in its tenuousness, who does not invest all meaning in it, who can most speak to it. Indeed, we suspect a little more sense of the frailty of human agendas might diminish the enthusiasm with which Christians rush to some offer of political salvation. While there have been times when great moral victories have been won in human crusades, far more have been the occasions when the dreams for which we risked all have turned out to be illusions.

## *A Permanent Remnant Psychology?*

Some Calvinist and Christian Reconstructionists have been critical of an emphasis on the suffering church as representing what one author called a dangerous "permanent-remnant psychology" which glories in failure and is incapable of bearing witness effectively to seek justice and God's order.

The Calvinist is right, we believe, in speaking about our public responsibility not only as citizens but as children of the Creator who is sovereign of all creation not just "religious" life. The mystery of his plan is that all creation will acknowledge him and live in unity with his Lordship. Pietism presents a danger in ignoring our responsibility as stewards and as members of our cultural and national communities. The nations, too, are part of God's plan. At the same time, we find the Anabaptist emphasis on expressing our public life in a manner consistent with the gentleness and powerlessness of our Lord to be a refreshing witness in a world gone mad with strategies for power and political machinations. In some strange, perhaps contradictory, way, the Anabaptist recognition of the critical question of *means* must be linked with the larger Catholic and Reformed traditions of *public ends*.

Certainly, notions of submission and non-resistance dare not silence the church. Submission is not withdrawal into pietism. It may even involve very vigorous insertion into the public order. Crosses do stand out against the landscape. Nor does submission mean that we are to hold in abeyance our moral convictions till majorities or principalities come to their senses. It does mean that all means of persuasion and witness must be measured by spiritual principles and not by utilitarian and narrow political factors. It insists that the character of the struggles in which we are engaged are spiritual and that the appropriate weapons must be chosen for such struggles.

For a people who live in the tradition of crosses and remnants, and who believe God called Israel and selected Bethlehem, the whole notion of victory and dominance will be a suspect category. The test of faithfulness for the biblical tradition will not be success. The conscientious dissenter has an advantage: winning, in a cultural sense, is not the objective. The dissenter is convinced that by his very refusal to cooperate he has already won. The state may grant an exemption or it may not, but the real battle was won when he said no. The politically or socially motivated disobedient, however, seeks precisely to get government to change its values and policies.

## Patience

Washington and Lee law professor Thomas Schaffer has suggested that the key to biblical faithfulness is not effectiveness, but patience. The martyrs, the witness of the Anabaptists, and our Lord's work on the cross are meaningless except in the context of hope, the conviction that the resurrection lies beyond the cross. Patience is recognizing the mystery of God's spirit working in our midst. It is knowing that our future is already in his hands. It is knowing his sovereignty and declining to usurp it.

This is not a patience of silence and fear. It is not a patience unaware of evil or one that is content to know that some day God will be the avenger. It is not a dulled conscience. Karl Barth spoke powerfully of the need to avoid that kind of false paralyzing patience: "We stand in need, not of patience, but of the impatience of the prophets, not of well mannered pleasantry, but of grim assault, not of the historian's balanced judgment. . . but of a love of truth that hacks its way through to the very backbone of the matter, and then dares to bring an accusation of unrighteousness against every upright man."

Biblical patience is waiting, trusting, hoping. It is knowing that all our works and labors may be fruitless. It is avoiding despair in the face of the despairing. But it is not simply a tactic of biding our time. North suggests: "A theology of perpetual patience is a theology which denies the necessity of an eventual confrontation."[4] Rather, any "period of patience must be a period of training."[5]

## Tactics

For all these reasons we believe that the issue of appropriate tactics in any civil resistance is as critical as that of the ends to be obtained. We note with alarm the rhetoric on the right of holy war. John Whitehead calls for "Christian rebels"; deception is praised as a biblically faithful tactic; Saul Alinsky's suggestions for creating havoc in the bureaucracy and Sun Tzu's military advice are praised; articles call for an armed citizenry; and one even suggests the use of underground radio. The tools for the struggle with the state are said to be video tape machines and lawsuits to intimidate public officials. A chain cutting tool becomes a key purchase. It all becomes a media event. As one volume suggests "Never forget, this is a war of public relations." Something seems tragically missing in all of that!

But equally so on the religious left, with their often arrogant confidence that they possess a truth which must be thrust upon the rest of us. If the demons of the right are courts, government bureaucrats, and internationalists, those of the left are industrialists and nationalists. Invading nuclear submarine bases to paint slogans on them, staging media events at the rotunda, and smuggling refugees from South America may be heroic and noble acts, but it is unclear that they are informed by Christian thought as to *means*.

The way to integrate biblical teaching about suffering and submission with our calling as stewards of the creation, doers of justice, and lovers of neighbors is not always clear. Biblical prophets may provide one model. They were a people who spoke boldly, declared God's judgment, feared no man or king, spoke about national life including politics, economics, and international affairs. While they had an intense experience of God, it drove them not from the world, but into it. Their holiness was deeply this-worldly. They often spoke in powerful symbols and dramatic acts. They were opposed by major religious and political elements.

Yet, when they spoke, they did so without political clout. They seemed to give little attention to alliances and constituents. They insisted that the word delivered was empowered. They were often ineffective, and some, like Jeremiah, were deeply broken by the blindness of the leadership. One, Ezekiel, was even told in advance he would be ignored. They were usually honored only posthumously. They offered their own people little hope of immediate victory, and certainly none based on clever political intrigue or military machinations.

Perhaps most significantly, they spoke chiefly to the houses of Israel and Judah. The place of the call for justice and righteousness was not primarily to Babylon or Egypt, but to the people of the covenant. It was there that the will of God was to be obeyed, and the faithful covenant-community established. It was the unfaithful community which was discrediting God and making his name a laughing-stock throughout the earth. The unfaithful community was also helpless to fulfill its mandate. But if that nation repented, trusted God, did justice at the gate, and befriended the stranger and sojourner—then *that* community could be a light to the nations, the people through whom all peoples would be blessed. Perhaps there is a model there.

*Canon: Individual conscience is an indispensable, but inadequate, guide to moral judgment and hence an insufficient basis for the moral justification of civil disobedience.*

A nation consisting of citizens whose consciences are bruised is itself broken in it national strength.

Abraham Kuyper

The emphasis on conscience as a guide to moral conduct, and the basis for civil disobedience is historic. It is the basis for distinguishing arguable civil disobedience from mere law-breaking. Abolitionist Theodore Parker spoke of conscience as the instrument by which we "learn justice." He declared in a pamphlet, that there are unchanging laws in the material and moral realm, laws "not made by men, but only discovered by them" and when confronted with unjust law, we are "no more morally bound to keep such rules of conduct, because King Pharaoh or King People say we shall, than the sun is materially bound to go around the earth every day, because Hipparchus and Ptolemy say it does." Conscience, Parker insisted, is the instrument by which we discover these eternal rules of conduct.

There is a claim of conscience upon us. Few are willing to accept the counsel of a soldier in *Henry V* who declares "we know enough if we know we are the King's subjects. If his cause is wrong, our obedience to the king wipes the crime of it out of us." Would that our consciences would allow such easy transfer of guilt. Eve (or the Devil) made me do it!

Generally, we admire people who act on their conscience. The elements of courage, risk, and integrity are impressive. In December 1970, Governor Winthrop Rockefeller of Arkansas, in commuting to life imprisonment the death sentences of fifteen prisoners, declared, "I cannot and will not turn my back on life-long Christian teachings and beliefs, merely to let history run out its course. . . . I could not live with myself."

In refusing to carry out orders for bombing missions in Vietnam, Captain Michael Heck wrote his parents: "I've taken a very drastic step. I've refused to take part in this war any longer. I cannot in good conscience be a part of it. . . . a man has to answer to himself first."

What is this thing called "conscience?" We are hard pressed to do much more than describe its consequences. Plutarch described conscience as "an ulcer in the flesh" which "never ceases to wound or goad" the soul. It is that sense which the Supreme Court noted in *Welsh* v. *U.S.*, when it declared that a violation of conscience "would give them no peace." Or as Shakespeare put it, "It fills a man full of obstacles." Its products are a sense of personal duty, guilt when ignored, perhaps even fear. It is the sense of lacking equilibrium, an absense of wholeness and integrity which we often refer to as a "guilty conscience."

Conscience is linked to our identity and integrity. One refuses to abide by the law in order to refuse to reorganize or renounce one's personal values and norms simply to conform to others. It is also highly individual, deeply personal. One's conscience is uniquely one's own. It is not worth much if you lease it out. Thoreau wondered why every man was given a conscience if his duty was to resign his own to the legislator's. In the seventeenth century, Governor Winthrop and Anne Hutchinson debated the question of the right to keep one's own conscience. Anne defended her practice of entertaining "saints" in her home by telling Winthrop, "That's a matter of conscience, sir." Winthrop, unmoved, replied, "Your conscience must be kept or it must be kept for you." And Anne replied, "Must not I then entertain the saints because I must keep my conscience?"

## *A Gift of God*

Encouraging persons to act consistent with the claims of conscience seems, in the main, a public benefit. Eric Fromm insists, "A sane society is one . . . where acting according to one's conscience is looked upon as a fundamental and necessary quality." Noted legal scholar Dworkin argues that the state has a general responsibility of leniency when someone acts out of conscience. James Childress declares, "It is prima facie a moral evil to force a person to act against his conscience."

Lord Morley suggested that the decline of a civilization is the consequence of a decline in the quality of conscience. Jurists Louis Brandeis and Oliver W. Holmes once suggested that a vital democracy required "courageous, self-reliant men (who do) not exalt order at the cost of liberty." Similarly, Ralph Templin notes that democracy is either realized or destroyed by "its defense or betrayal in its place of inner integrity: the conscience of man."

The concept of conscience is likewise evident in scripture. The very concept of man as a being with a moral consciousness implies at least a capacity of moral assessment. Though the Old Testament does not use the word directly, it is implied in many stories such as the account of Cain and Abel. Capacities for moral action and guilt are implied long before the law is given at Sinai. Abraham expresses concern for his life because others seem to have no conscience, because "the fear of God is not in this place" (Gn 20:11). The prophet Jeremiah spoke of a "law in their inward parts" and written on their hearts. There is the repeated notation that someone "feared God" (e.g., Dt 25:18).

In the New Testament, Paul uses the word conscience twenty-three times, and it seems assumed in passages such as Romans 2:1-15. Paul points to a basic awareness in man, apart from revelation, of right and wrong. The failure of persons to act in accord with conscience, with the light they have, is the cause of their demise.

Advocates of civil resistance appeal to conscience as both a motive and justification, and urge others to listen to their hearts. One publication calling for anti-war resistance challenged readers to fill the jails and provide the nation "the slap of conscience it so desperately needs." Nevertheless, notwithstanding our praise of inner promptings and the maintenance of integrity, there are serious limits to the trustworthiness of conscience.

*As a guide to moral judgment, conscience is far too subjective.* Despite our tendency to affirm the presence of conscience, its moral character, and the duty to obey it, Hannah Arendt was surely correct when she spoke of the "anarchic nature of divinely inspired conscience." Thoreau's individualism seems courageous: "I think that it is enough if they have God on their side, without waiting for that other one." The problem with the private inner light and vision is that often the assumption is that it is the voice of God, light, and goodness. But what if it is, instead, a heart of darkness? Judge Frank Johnson observed that "the man who chooses to disobey the law on principle may be a saint, but he may also be a madman."

The scriptures note the potential for conscience to be seared, or to lose its moral content by persistence in evil to the point that it actually endorses and sanctions the evil (Rom 1).

The subjectivity and ambiguity of conscience was dramatically suggested by Truman Nelson: "One can be an individual like John Bunyan and sit in jail for acting against the State and write *Pilgrim's Progress*, or, like Hitler, write *Mein Kampf*."[6] Christian philosophers have universally concurred. Augustine said conscience was a "subordinate authority" which might need to yield to a higher authority. Conscience was subject to the correction of higher authority or law. Aquinas agreed, though he did insist that if the conscience persisted to call one to act contrary to the counsel of others, one had a duty to avoid sin and follow the subjective conscience: "As far as lies within him, a man (who has heard the voice of conscience but chooses to disobey it) is determined not to obey the will of God."

*As a basis for the moral justification of civil disobedience, conscience confuses motive with justification, personal morality with objective morality.* It is often suggested that not only ought leniency be granted to the conscientious objectors, but that the sincerity of the actors, their conscientiousness, somehow makes it morally right. Of course, their conscience does make it clear that it is morally right—to *them*. But is that relevant objectively?

Sincerity and conscientiousness are largely "red herrings" in the question of the moral defensibility of an act of civil disobedience. Acts of civil disobedience are properly "holy" not solely on the basis on what inner light reveals. Joseph Sax has properly noted that one may be as committed and sincere about exterminating Jews as about ending wars: "It is not the sincerity that counts, but the justness of one's goals and the appropriateness of the means chosen to reach them."[7]

*In exaggerated forms, the focus on individual conscience may even produce an irrational and dangerous type of holy disobedience.* While we rightly honor the person who wishes to obey the call of God, it is equally apparent that not all who claim to have heard the call are hearing the right voices. One author has spoken of the special problems created by the religious zealot, those "immersed in a crusade, motivated by a sense of outrage and injustice, and sometimes by a messianic vision." There is a potential danger in the religious conscience, the inner voice, the individualistic perspective. The voice of conscience may mask illusion and neuroses, or it may color truth with an irrational zeal that ceases to weigh the significance of means.

Laraine Fergensen has written of the dangers of what she calls "transcendental politics" and the "moral superiority" characteristic of civil disobedience rooted in individualistic religious conscience—a superiority which may insulate from the truth sought.[8] This seems especially a threat where the civil disobedience is undertaken not merely to be excused from a claim—direct conscientious disobedience, but where the disobedient seeks to move the social or political order. Nothing can be quite so dangerous as one who believes he or she has been called to save us from ourselves, and will insist on doing so.

Fergensen cites Daniel Berrigan as a classic illustration of conscience run to egotism and delusion. Noting Berrigan's attack on Israel as "a criminal Jewish community" dominated by entrepreneurs, millionaires, and generals, Fergensen wonders whether often "the inner light . . . does not become a dangerously blinding glare." Not all with the prophet's rhetoric possess his righteousness. Berrigan was assuming the part of the biblical prophet "with all of the rage, but none of the wisdom or truth of an Isaiah or a Jeremiah."[9]

There is also a tendency for religiously inspired disobedients to engage in the political process with an enormous degree of self-righteousness. The very clarity of their vision comes as a demand to the political process. They come speaking of "witness" and "consciousness raising," but when that has failed, they persist in their demands that the public order still accept their vision. One commentator warned that such persons lack a necessary pragmatic ethic which permits the sort of give and take necessary in the political process:

One must possess a readiness to be content with compromises . . . however sound his convictions may seem to him. This readiness will be difficult if one's disobedience is allowed to become too much an expression of righteous indignation at unjust laws. Those who engage in their civil disobedience mainly as such an expression will tend to give their causes peculiarly moral or religious airs and so turn their struggle into a "holy" crusade, claiming the "unconditional surrender" of their opponents as the only right end, and therefore regarding any thought of compromise as an immoral "sell out."[10]

### Not Only a Higher Law, but a Broader Community

While acting in accord with the moral claims of one's conscience is a prerequisite if civil disobedience is to be holy, it is not a sufficient condition. Conscience is too subject to the vagaries of personal psychological life as well as social and political history to be trustworthy.

Conscience must itself be weighed by something other than its own rhythm. It is not self-authenticating. Civil disobedience's link to conscience must be to "a grander rhythm of conscientious history."

The word itself which originally meant joint knowledge suggests that conscience properly understood is not to be a self-generated monitor, but rather a product of a morally sensitive community. As Konvitz notes regarding the Jewish tradition, conscience was not a voice that speaks from man, but a hearing agency for the voice of God. It is not being true to oneself, but to the more objective referent of God's will. It is not a private law, but an appropriation of the word of God. Conscience does not make law. It has a reporting not an originating function.

Conscience-creating and shaping, then, is the work of the ministry of the church. We do not simply expect others to submit to our conscience, but equally we must submit it to review.

"In the counsel of many there is wisdom," Proverbs tells us. But it is more than mere numbers that the church offers. It is the collective wisdom of the church under the Spirit of God. "No Scripture is of any private interpretation," the scriptures warn us. In the individualism rampant in American religious, as well as economic and political, life, such a reality check is critical.

The church must also be understood not only in the sense of my immediate Christian fellowship, but in the more biblical sense of the whole church across time. With the American tendency to select churches that are comfortable, sociologically and ideologically, it is too easy to assure support for one's views, regardless of orientation, by merely gathering around ourselves those who agree. By an openness to the church at large, we must hear also the counsel and wisdom of many voices. The history of Christian faithfulness and witness now becomes part of the counsel.

Of course, candor requires that we acknowledge that the collectivity of the church has often itself been deluded by the cultural or governmental ethos. The church itself may be badly divided as it has been on such public issues today as abortion, nuclear armaments, the Vietnam War, and even on civil disobedience itself. The prophetic tradition is, to some extent, a recognition that the established structures of religion may miss, tragically, a central claim of God. It is the task of the minority, often of very small minorities, to speak not simply to government but to the church.

Were prophets to be silent merely because their institutional colleagues counseled restraint, we would have lost the powerful witness of Elijah and Amos. Modern prophets and spokesmen like Luther, Gandhi, King, and Bonhoeffer often acted without strong institutional church endorsement.

Bedau once made the point clearly that not every claim of conscience is entitled to our moral approbation: "It does not follow from the fact that a man cannot do more than whatever he thinks he ought to do, that he ought to do whatever he thinks he ought to do."[11]

"Civil disobedience, like law itself, is habit forming, and the habit it forms is destructive of law." So observed Harvard law professor Alexander Bickel.

Indeed it is, and Bickel, like others, is nervous about individuals appropriating to themselves decisions about obeying the law. In *Leviathan*, Hobbes warned that under such a regime "every man would be a wolf to anothers." John Rawls said that disobedience violates the "duty of fair play" to one another in a democratic and constitutional society.

The consequences of such a "habit" may be disastrous. Howard Zinn writing in *The Nation* likened civil disobedience to a "tiny hole in a dike; the rationales rush through like a torrent." Even Justice Black warned that today's "crowd moved by noble ideals" will tomorrow be "a mob ruled by hate and passion and greed and violence."

But there is another "habit" even more ominous, and we believe ultimately more destructive—the habit of moral abdication, of atrophied consciences for lack of exercise, the waiver of moral decision-making. Not only for our souls, but for our culture, we dare not lose the capacity for asking questions which probe deeper than the statute books and the products of the political processes and judicial fiats.

The habit of moral evaluation cannot be leased or surrendered, even to enlighted representatives. The moral life thrives in a nation, not by investing it in the few, but by cultivating its broad exercise.

Nor must the habit of a morally active conscience simply be cultivated. There are times when that conscience compels courageous action. Morality must be more than reflection, it must also be action. It is inherently witness, it demands incarnation. It thrives on consistency. As the noted legal philosopher H.L.A. Hart warned, there is always the "danger that existing law may supplant morality as a final test of conduct."

For believers, the test of conduct is never law alone. There is another claim, another duty, and there are times when that claim is of such a nature that obedience to it requires the courage, the risk, and perhaps the suffering of a firm *no* to the law. In fact, it was Gandhi who insisted that "when neglect of the call means a denial of God, civil disobedience becomes a peremptory duty."

# Notes

## Chapter One
## Holy Disobedience

1. Francis Schaeffer, *A Christian Manifesto* (Westchester, Ill.: Crossways Books, Good News Publishing Co., 1981), p. 110.
2. Franky Schaeffer, *A Time for Anger: The Myth of Neutrality* (Westchester, Ill.: Crossway Books, 1982).
3. Judge Randall Hekman, "Letter to the Editor," *Grand Rapids Press*, November 19, 1982.
4. Kent Kelly, *The Separation of Church and Freedom* (South Pines: Calvary, 1980), p. 234.
5. Francis Schaeffer, quoted in John W. Whitehead, "Resistance in the Face of State Interference," in *Theology of Christian Resistance*, ed. Gary North, (Tyler, Tex.: Geneva Divinity School Press, 1983), p. 3.
6. *Christian Manifesto*, p. 130.
7. Allen Stang, "What the War Is Really About," *The Theology of Christian Resistance*, p. 24.
8. Ibid., p. 38.
9. Rousas Rushdoony, "Religious Liberty versus Religious Toleration," *Tactics of Christian Resistance* (Tyler, Tex.: Geneva Divinity School Press, 1983), p. 34.
10. Gary North and David Chilton, "Apologetics and Strategy," *Tactics of Christian Resistance*, p. 138.
11. Jim Wallis, "A Higher Loyalty," *Sojourners* (May 1983), p. 4.
12. John K. Stoner, "The Moral Equivalent of Disarmament," *Sojourners* (February 1979), p. 15.
13. William Durland, "Paying For Peace," *Sojourners* (February 1979).
14. Jim Wallis, "A Dream," *Sojourners* (August 1980), p. 3.
15. Ched Myers, "Storming the Gates of Hell," *Christian Century* (September 16, 1981), p. 898.
16. Quoted in Dean Snyder, "Civil Disobedience: What It Means," *Christian Century* (April 27, 1983), p. 403.

## Chapter Two
## What's Going On Here?

1. George Will, *Statecraft as Soulcraft: What Government Does* (New York: Simon & Schuster, 1983).

2. Richard Niebuhr, *Christ and Culture* (New York: Harper & Row, 1951), pp. 8, 9.
3. Harold Berman, *Law and Revolution: The Formation of the Western Legal Tradition,* vol. 2 (Cambridge, Mass.: Harvard University Press, 1983), p. 39.
4. Jacques Ellul, *Theological Foundation of the Law* (New York: Seabury Press, 1960), p. 31.
5. *The Dialogues of Plato,* ed. B. Jowett, vol. 1 (1937), p. 434.

## Chapter Three
### Definitions: A Rose by Any Other Name . . .

1. Morris Keeton, "The Morality of Civil Disobedience," *Texas Law Review* 43 (1965), p. 508.
2. Lewis Feuer, "On Civil Disobedience, 1967," *New York Times Magazine* (November 26, 1967), p. 29.
3. Hugo Bedau, "On Civil Disobedience," *Journal of Philosophy* 58 (1961), p. 659.
4. Martin Luther King, "Letter from a Birmingham Jail," *Sojourners* (May 1983), p. 19.
5. Hugo Bedau, "On Civil Disobedience," *Journal of Philosophy* 58(1961), p. 660.
6. Howard Zinn, *Disobedience and Democracy* (New York: Vintage, 1968), p. 30.
7. Carl Cohen, "Civil Disobedience: Moral or Not," *The Nation* (December 2, 1968), p. 599.
8. Zinn, *Disobedience and Democracy,* p. 30.
9. Carl Cohen, "Essence and Ethics of Civil Disobedience," *Nation* (March 16, 1964), p. 257.
10. Weingartner, "Justifying Civil Disobedience," *Columbia University Forum* (Spring 1966), p. 38.
11. Gene Sharp, "A Study of the Meanings of Non-Violence II," *Gandhi Marg* (January 1960), p. 1.
12. Fred Berger, "Obligation in Disobedience: A Study of the Justification of Civil Disobedience in the Democratic State" (Ph.D. dissertation, University of California, Berkeley, 1966), p. 54.

## Chapter Four
### Civil Disobedience: As American As Apple Pie

1. Gary F. Herschberger, *Nonresistance and the State,* p. 94.
2. David R. Weber, *Civil Disobedience in American History* (Ithaca, N.Y.: Cornell University Press, 1978), p. 94.
3. Ibid., p. 95.
4. Ibid., p. 237.
5. Staughton Lynd, ed., *Nonviolence in America* (New York: Bobbs-Merrill, 1968), p. 260.

6. Weber, *Civil Disobedience in American History*, p. 244.
7. Staughton, *Nonviolence in America*, p. 464.
8. Ibid., p. 378.
9. Weber, *Civil Disobedience in American History*, p. 284.

## Chapter Five
### Thoreau, Gandhi, and King: The Legacy of Creative Protest

1. Dale W. Brown, *Spiritual and Intellectual Roots* (Berea, Ky.: Berea College Press, 1982), p. 15.
2. Henry S. Canby, *Thoreau* (Boston: Houghton Mifflin Co., 1939), p. 233.
3. Henry David Thoreau, "Civil Disobedience," in *Walden, and Civil Disobedience,* ed. Owen Thomas, p. 224.
4. Thoreau, "Civil Disobedience," p. 227.
5. Martin Luther King, *Stride Toward Freedom: The Montgomery Story* (New York: Harper and Row, Perennial Library, 1964).
6. Thoreau, "Civil Disobedience," p. 236.
7. Jerome Lawrence and Robert Lee, *The Night Thoreau Spent in Jail* (New York: Hill & Wang, 1971), p. vii.
8. Richard Grenier, "The Gandhi Nobody Knows," *Commentary* (March 1983), p. 59.
9. Mohandas K. Gandhi, *Non-Violent Resistance* (New York: Schocken Books, 1961), p. 77.
10. Ibid., p. 140.
11. Ibid., p. 173.
12. Calvin Kytle, *Gandhi, Soldier of Non-Violence* (Cabin John, Md.: Seven Locks Press, 1982), p. 150.
13. Gandhi, *Non-Violent Resistance*, p. 170.
14. King, *Stride,* p. 96.
15. Jim Wallace, "From Protest to Resistance," *Sojourners* (February 1984), p. 3.
16. Martin Luther King, *Strength to Love* (New York: William Collins & World Publishing Co., 1963), p. 14.
17. King, *Stride,* p. 101.
18. Lerone Bennett, *What Manner of Man* (Chicago: Johnson Publishing Co., 1964), p. 4.
19. King, *Stride,* pp. 19-31, passim.
20. Ibid., p. 14.
21. David R. Weber, *Civil Disobedience in American History* (Ithaca, N.Y.: Cornell University Press, 1978), p. 212.
22. King, *Strength,* p. 54.
23. Ibid., p. 132.
24. King, "Letter from a Birmingham Jail," p. 19.
25. King, *Strength,* p. 33.
26. King, "Letter," p. 19.
27. Ibid.

28. Bennett, *What Manner,* p. 198.
29. Jim Bishop, *The Days of Martin Luther King* (New York: G.P. Putnam's Sons, 1971), p. 193.
30. Bennett, *What Manner,* p. 135.

## Chapter Six
### Holy Disobedience: A Christian Tradition

1. H. Richard Niebuhr, *Christ and Culture* (New York: Harper and Row, 1951), p. 1.
2. Ibid., p. 7.
3. Ibid., p. 8.
4. Ernst Troeltsch, *The Social Teaching of the Christian Church,* vol. 1 (Chicago: University of Chicago Press, 1981), p. 87.
5. Umphrey Lee, *The Historic Church and Modern Pacifism* (New York: Abingdon-Cokesbury Press), p. 53.
6. Jean-Michel Hornus, *It Is Not Lawful for Me to Fight,* Scottsdale, Penn.: Herald Press, 1980) p. 138.
7. Daniel B. Stevick, *Civil Disobedience and the Christian* (New York: Seabury Press, 1969), p. 49.
8. Troeltsch, *Social Teaching,* p. 315.
9. Thomas Aquinas, *Summa Theologica* IaIIae, q. 96, art. 4.
10. Lee, *Historic Church,* p. 86.
11. Martin Marty, "Baptistification Takes Over (a Baptist Style of Christian Life)," *Christianity Today* (September 2, 1983), pp. 33-36.
12. Theodore Tappert, *Selected Writings of Martin Luther* (Philadelphia: Fortress Press, 1967), pp. 280-81.
13. Niebuhr, *Christ and Culture,* p. 188.
14. Luther, as quoted in *Civil Disobedience,* p. 57.

## Chapter Seven
### Modern Religious Voices

1. Thomas A. Shannon, *Render unto God: A Theology of Selective Obedience* (New York: Paulist Press, 1974), p. 54.
2. Ibid., p. 56.
3. Latin American bishops, quoted by Gustavo Gutierrez, "Hope of Liberation," *Mission Trends No. 3, Third World Theologies,* ed. Gerald Anderson (New York: Paulist, 1976), p. 66.
4. Gustavo Gutierrez, "Liberation Theology," quoted by Neuhaus in *Mission Trends No. 3* (Grand Rapids, Mich.: Wm. B. Eerdmans Publishing Co., 1976), p.53.
5. Jose Miguez Bonino, "Violence: A Theological Reflection," in *Mission Trends, No. 3* p. 120.
6. Neuhaus *Mission Trends, No. 3* p. 61.
7. Dietrich Bonhoeffer, *Ethics* (New York: Macmillan, 1965), p. 209.
8. Ibid., p. 350.

9. Ibid.
10. John Howard Yoder, *The Christian Witness to the State* (Newton, Kans.: Faith & Life Press, 1969), p. 22.
11. Ibid., p. 50.
12. Ibid., p. 54.
13. Jim Wallis, "A Higher Loyalty," *Sojourners* (May 1983), p. 3.
14. Francis Nigel Lee, "The Christian Manifesto of 1984," *Tactics of Christian Resistance* (Tyler, Tex.: Geneva Divinity School Press, 1983), p. 11.
15. Gary North and David Chilton, "Apologetics and Strategy," *Tactics of Christian Resistance,* pp. 127-28.
16. Francis Schaeffer, *The Christian Manifesto* (Westchester, Ill.: Good News Publishers, 1981), p. 121.
17. Ibid., p. 130.

## Chapter Eight
### Render unto Caesar: Scripture and Obedience

1. J.W. Allen, *A History of Political Thought in the Sixteenth Century* (London: Methuen & Co., 1928), p. 132.
2. Clinton Morrison, *The Powers That Be* (Naperville, Ill.: A.A. Allenson, 1960), p. 106.
3. William Stringfellow, *Conscience and Obedience: The Politics of Romans 13 and Revelation 13 in Light of the Second Coming* (Waco, Tex.: Word Publishers, 1977), p. 35.
4. John Stoner, "The Moral Equivalent of Disarmament," *Sojourners* (February 1979).
5. Vernard Eller, "That the Old May Be Judged," *Brethren Life and Thought* (Spring 1974).
6. Morrison, *Powers That Be,* p. 29.
7. Daniel Daube, *Civil Disobedience in Antiquity* (Edinburgh: Edinburgh University Press, 1972), p. 5.
8. Ched Myers, "By What Authority," *Sojourners* (May 1983), p. 12.
9. Daube, *Civil Disobedience in Antiquity,* p. 82.
10. Daniel Stevick, *Civil Disobedience and the Christian* (New York: Seabury Press, 1969).

## Chapter Nine
### Civil Disobedience and the Law: Loopholes and Principles

1. Daniel Berrigan, "Two Commandments for Law Breakers," *Christianity and Crisis* (April 27, 1981), p. 116.
2. Thomas Rekdal, "Civil Disobedience as a Constitutional Problem" (Ph.D. dissertation, University of Washington, 1975), p. 17.
3. Harrop Freeman, "Civil Disobedience, Law and Democracy, III," *Law in Transition* (Winter 1966).
4. Freeman, "Civil Disobedience," p. 14.

5. Robert McKay, "Protest and Dissent: Action and Reaction," *Utah Law Review* 25 (1966).
6. Rekdal, "Civil Disobedience as a Constitutional Problem," p. 43.
7. Ronald Dworkin, "On Not Prosecuting Civil Disobedience," *New York Review of Books* (June 6, 1968).
8. Rekdal, "Civil Disobedience as a Constitutional Problem," p. 7.
9. Robert Hall, "Legal Toleration of Civil Disobedience," *Ethics* 81 (1971), p. 128.
10. Jerome Frank, *Law and the Modern Mind* (New York: Garden City, N.Y.: Doubleday, Anchor Books, 1963), pp. 330-35.
11. Bill Ourland, "Case Denied," *Sojourners* (March 1980), pp. 8-11.
12. Melanie Morrison, "As One Who Stands Convicted," *Sojourners* (May 1979), p. 15.
13. Daniel Berrigan, "Two Commandments," *Christianity and Crisis* (April 27, 1981), p. 120.
14. Harrop Freeman, "Moral Preemption Part I: The Case for the Disobedient," *Hastings Law Journal* 17 (March 1966), p. 428.
15. Nancy Ellen Abrams, "Nuclear War," *California Lawyer* (February 1983), pp. 25-28, 67.
16. Charles Rice, "Civil Disobedience: Formula for Chaos," *Alabama Lawyer* 27 (1966), p. 248.
17. Louis Waldman, "Civil Rights, Yes; Civil Disobedience, No," *New York State Bar Journal* (August 1965), pp. 331, 334-35.
18. Ernest van den Haag, "Civil Disobedience and the Law," *Rutgers Law Review* 21 (Fall 1966), p. 40.
19. "Moral Preemption," p. 434.
20. Bertrand Russell, *Autobiography of Bertrand Russell*, vol. 3 (New York: Simon & Schuster, 1969), pp. 194, 197, 198.

## Chapter Ten
### Civil Disobedience and the Free Exercise of Religion

1. Morris Clark, "Guidelines for the Free Exercise Clause," *Harvard Law Review* 83 (1969), pp. 327, 336-37.
2. Ibid., p. 336.
3. Harrop Freeman, "A Remonstrance for Conscience," 56 *University of Pennsylvania Law Review* 56 (1956), p. 826.
4. "Guidelines," p. 337.
5. James F. Childress, "Appeals to Conscience," 89 *Ethics* (1979), p. 315.
6. Donald Gianella, "Religious Liberty, Non-Establishment and Doctrinal Development: Part I. The Religions Liberty Guarantee," *Harvard Law Review* 80 (1967), pp. 1381, 1890.

## Chapter Eleven
### The Bottom Line

1. Mary Lou Kownaki, "A Member of a Religious Community," in *Peacemakers* (New York: Harper & Row, 1983).

2. Herbert Schlossberg, *Idols of Destruction* (Nashville: Thomas Nelson, 1983), p. 304.
3. David Burrell and Stanley Hauerwas, quoted in T. Schaffer, *On Being a Christian and Being a Lawyer* (Provo, Utah: Brigham Young University Press), p. 20.
4. *Theology of Christian Resistance,* Gary North, ed. (Tyler, Tex.: Geneva Divinity School Press, 1983), p. 56.
5. Ibid., p. 61.
6. Truman Nelson, "Thoreau and John Brown," in *Thoreau in Our Season,* ed. John Hicks (Boston: University of Massachusetts Press, 1966), p. 138.
7. Joseph Sax, "Civil Disobedience and the Law," *Current* (November 1968), p. 10.
8. Laraine Fergenson, "Thoreau, Daniel Berrigan and the Problem of Transcendental Politics," *Soundings* 65 (Spring 1982), p. 103.
9. Ibid., p. 113.
10. Harry Prosch, "Toward an Ethic of Civil Disobedience," *Ethics* 77 (April 1967), p. 189.
11. Bedau, "On Civil Disobedience," *Journal of Philosophy* 58 (1961), pp. 653, 663.

# Index

# DATE DUE

| | | | |
|---|---|---|---|
| Phillips JAN 11 1985 | | | |
| Phillips OCT 14 1996 | | | |
| | | | |
| | | | |
| | | | |
| | | | |
| | | | |
| | | | |
| | | | |
| | | | |
| | | | |
| | | | |
| | | | |
| | | | |
| | | | |
| | | | |

HIGHSMITH 45-102                    PRINTED IN U.S.A.